AS/A Level

THE KITE RUNNER

KHALED HOSSEINI

Oxford
Literature
Companions

Notes and activities: Garrett O'Doherty
Series consultant: Peter Buckroyd

OXFORD
UNIVERSITY PRESS

Contents

Themes 78

Critical Views 92

Skills and Practice 104

Glossary 118

Introduction

What are Oxford Literature Companions?

Oxford Literature Companions is a series designed to provide you with comprehensive support for popular set texts. You can use the Companion alongside your play, using relevant sections during your studies or using the book as a whole for revision.

Each Companion includes detailed guidance and practical activities on:

- **Plot and Structure**
- **Context**
- **Genre**
- **Characterisation and Roles**
- **Language**
- **Themes**
- **Performance**
- **Critical Views**
- **Skills and Practice**

How does this book help with exam preparation?

As well as providing guidance on key areas of the play, throughout this book you will also find 'Upgrade' features. These are tips to help with your exam preparation and performance.

In addition, in the extensive **Skills and Practice** chapter, the 'Exam skills' section provides detailed guidance on areas such as how to prepare for the exam, understanding the question, planning your response and hints for what to do (or not do) in the exam.

In the **Skills and Practice** chapter there is also a bank of **Sample questions** and **Sample answers**. The **Sample answers** are marked and include annotations and a summative comment.

How does this book help with terminology?

Throughout the book, key terms are **highlighted** in the text and explained on the same page. There is also a detailed **Glossary** at the end of the book that explains, in the context of the play, all the relevant literary terms highlighted in this book.

Which edition of the play has this book used?

Quotations and character names have been taken from the Bloomsbury edition of The Kite Runner (ISBN 978-140-882485-6).

How does this book work?

Each book in the Oxford Literature Companions series follows the same approach and includes the following features:

- **Key quotations** from the play
- **Key terms** explained on the page and linked to a complete glossary at the end of the book
- **Activity boxes** to help improve your understanding of the text
- **Upgrade** tips to help prepare you for your assessment

Upgrade tips to help prepare you for your assessment

Key quotations from the play

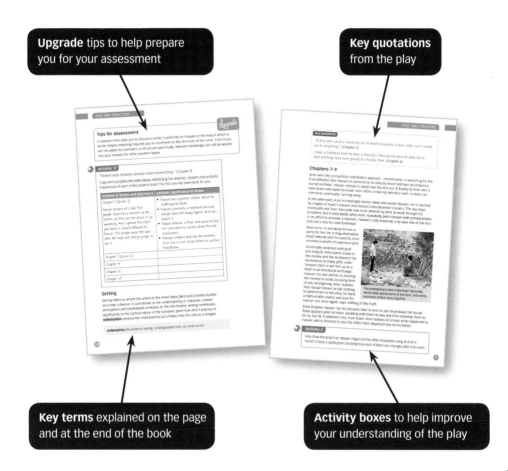

Key terms explained on the page and at the end of the book

Activity boxes to help improve your understanding of the play

Plot and Structure

Plot

Chapters 1–6

It is December 2001 and Amir, an Afghan immigrant living in San Francisco, reflects on a phone call that he took the previous summer from Rahim Khan, a family friend in Pakistan. It prompts Amir to think about his former life in Kabul, the capital of Afghanistan, and a childhood incident in 1975. He confesses that the incident 'changed everything' *(Chapter 1)*.

Amir, whose mother died giving birth to him, describes a comfortable life growing up in an affluent Kabul suburb with his father, Baba. The latter is a physically powerful, charismatic and successful businessman. Ali, a servant, and his son Hassan are employed to do menial chores. They live in the grounds of the house in a basic hut but their connection to the family is a strong one, dating back to the time Amir's grandfather adopted the orphaned Ali.

Amir and Hassan are very good friends; Amir carves their names in a pomegranate tree in a declaration of friendship. They share certain experiences too. For example, Hassan's mother Sanaubar abandoned him and his father less than a week after giving birth. However, a profound social and religious divide exists between Amir and Hassan. Baba and Amir are of the majority ethnic group, Pashtun, and are therefore Sunni Muslims, while Ali and Hassan are from the minority ethnic group, Hazara, and are therefore Shi'a Muslims.

One night, Amir overhears Baba confess his shame to Rahim Khan that his son is so unlike him; instead, Amir is a cowardly boy with an interest in books and writing. Baba is frustrated that Amir must be defended from the other children by Hassan. In one such instance, Hassan threatens the violent local bully, Assef, with his slingshot. Amir admits to a deep alienation from his father and a growing sense of jealousy towards Hassan when Baba is kind to him. In fits of envy, Amir sporadically exploits Hassan's lack of education to ridicule him.

Politically, things change when King Mohammed Zahir Shah is overthrown and a republic with a new president is declared. When Hassan's birthday arrives, Baba gifts him plastic surgery to correct his cleft lip. With winter comes the annual kite season and an opportunity for Amir to impress his father in a major competition. He is an accomplished kite flyer and Hassan is renowned as the best kite runner, the individual who chases after and catches the defeated kites.

Activity 1

a) How is Amir's character revealed in these early chapters?

b) Make a list of the key events in the plot that impact on Amir. Identify whether they are positive or negative. Choose a short quotation that shows the effect of each event.

Chapters 7–9

Amir wins the competition and Baba's approval – momentarily. In searching for the final defeated kite, Hassan is cornered in an alley by Assef and two accomplices, Kamal and Wali. Hassan refuses to hand over the kite out of loyalty to Amir and is held down and raped by Assef. Amir hides, cowering behind a wall. He does not intervene, eventually running away.

In the aftermath, Amir increasingly cannot sleep and avoids Hassan. He is haunted by images of Assef's assault and Hassan's bloodstained trousers. The two boys eventually visit their favourite tree in an attempt by Amir to work through his emotions, but it ends badly when Amir repeatedly pelts Hassan with pomegranates in an effort to provoke a reaction. Hassan's only response is to take one of the fruit and rub it into his own forehead.

Amir turns 13 and Baba throws a party for him. He is disgusted when Assef attends with his parents. Amir receives a wealth of expensive gifts.

Continually wracked with guilt and disgust, Amir plants some of the money and the wristwatch he received as birthday gifts under Hassan's bed to set him up as a thief. In an emotional exchange, Hassan lies and admits to stealing the money to avoid accusing Amir of any wrongdoing. Amir realises that Hassan knows he did nothing to defend him in the alley. He feels unfathomable shame and love for Hassan but, once again, says nothing of the truth.

The pomegranate tree is the boys' favourite, where they spend some of the best, and worst, moments of their lives together

Baba forgives Hassan, but Ali declares that he and his son must leave the house. Baba appears grief-stricken, pleading with them to stay and then ordering them to do so, but Ali is adamant they must leave. Amir realises Ali knows what happened to Hassan and is shocked to see the effect their departure has on his father.

Activity 2

How does the attack on Hassan impact on the other characters living at Amir's home? Create a spidergram showing how each of their lives changes after this event.

Key quotations

And that right there was the single greatest moment of my twelve years of life, seeing Baba on that roof, proud of me at last. *(Chapter 7)*

I could step into that alley, stand up for Hassan—the way he'd stood up for me all those times in the past—and accept whatever would happen to me. Or I could run. In the end, I ran. *(Chapter 7)*

Hassan milled about the periphery of my life after that. I made sure our paths crossed as little as possible... *(Chapter 8)*

Then I saw Baba do something I had never seen him do before: He cried. *(Chapter 9)*

Chapters 10–14

Afghanistan is invaded by the Soviets (from the USSR, now Russia) in 1979. Baba and 18-year-old Amir flee to Jalalabad in a truck with a people smuggler called Karim to escape the violence. En route, Baba risks his life to defend a woman from the unwanted sexual advances of a Russian soldier and later attacks Karim when he cannot take them further as he had promised. They spend a week in a dirty, rat-infested basement until they can be transported to Pakistan. Present with them is Kamal, who held Hassan down while Assef raped him. He appears lifeless and his father reveals that his son has been raped, ironically. The refugees flee Jalalabad in an empty fuel truck. On arrival in Peshawar, Kamal is dead and, in his grief, his father shoots himself.

Six months later, Baba and Amir are living in Fremont, California. Baba works at a petrol station and Amir studies English at high school. On his graduation day, Baba is proud and buys Amir, now 20, a car. The experience is ruined for Amir when Baba announces, "I wish Hassan had been with us today" *(Chapter 11)*. Amir embraces America more easily than his father. They earn extra money by buying and selling things at a local flea market that is dominated by the many Afghans who have sought refuge in the area. It is here that Amir meets his future wife Soraya.

Soraya's father, General Taheri, is a strict Afghan who expects Amir to court his daughter in the traditional way. When Baba is diagnosed with cancer, Amir asks him to approach Soraya's father so that their courtship can begin. Soraya is eager to tell Amir of her past, as she had lived previously with an Afghan man with whom she had run away. In traditional Afghan culture, this makes Soraya undesirable as a potential wife, but it does not deter Amir. Due to Baba's illness, their courtship and engagement is brief and they soon marry. Shortly after this, Baba dies.

The young couple settle into married life and Amir studies English at university. He does not return to the flea market. In 1989, his first book is published. Soraya is infertile, which Amir feels is a punishment for his past sins. A second book is published and they move to San Francisco, into a bigger house. Amir and Soraya have been married for 15 years when Rahim Khan telephones to ask Amir to visit him in Pakistan.

Activity 3

Why is Kamal, who has suffered the same assault as Hassan, reintroduced at this point of the story?

Key quotations

For me, America was a place to bury my memories. For Baba, a place to mourn his. *(Chapter 11)*

Lying awake in bed that night, I thought of Soraya [...] My heart stuttered at the thought of her. *(Chapter 11)*

...perhaps something, someone, somewhere, had decided to deny me fatherhood for the things I had done. *(Chapter 13)*

Chapters 15–18

Amir makes the journey to Pakistan to see Rahim Khan, who reveals that he is dying and has a favour to ask. He explains that he lived in Baba's house after Baba and Amir fled from Kabul, intending to look after it, believing that Baba would return. Waves of violence and conflict, he says, destroyed the city and the country. Feeling lonely and requiring help, Rahim Khan sought out Ali and Hassan in 1986. He found Hassan, happily married and living a humble life in a mud house, but Ali had been killed two years previously. Hassan eventually agrees to move back to Kabul with his wife, Farzana, and Rahim Khan, but he refuses to sleep in the house and reverts to the basic hut he previously shared with his father. He and Farzana lose their first child; then his mother Sanaubar unexpectedly reappears one day. She is desperately weak and her face has been badly mutilated. Although she abandoned him, Hassan forgives her and takes her in. She subsequently delivers Hassan's firstborn son Sohrab in 1990.

Despite the violence, Rahim Khan paints a picture of domestic happiness within the confines of the house and explains that Hassan was a devoted father. Sanaubar dies in her sleep in 1994. Rahim Khan gives Amir a letter and a photo from Hassan and then reveals that Hassan and his wife were brutally killed by the Taliban.

It is Rahim Khan's wish that Amir go to Kabul and get Hassan's son from an orphanage so that he can be placed in the care of a local foster family. Amir rejects the idea but is stunned to learn that he and Hassan were half-brothers. The revelation that Baba fathered Hassan and kept it secret from him leaves Amir confused and angry. Encouraged by Rahim Khan to see this as an opportunity to atone (make amends) for all past sins, Amir agrees to go and save the boy.

Activity 4

Amir's relationship with Baba is an important one and contributes significantly to the plot. What other father/son relationships exist in the novel and how do these relationships reflect and develop that of Amir and Baba?

Activity 5

Explain the purpose of Sanaubar in relation to the plot of the novel.

Key quotations

"I'm thirty-eight years old and I've just found out my whole life is one big fucking lie!" *(Chapter 17)*

As it turned out, Baba and I were more alike than I'd ever known […] Rahim Khan had summoned me here to atone not just for my sins but for Baba's too. *(Chapter 18)*

Tips for assessment

It is vital that you know the plot thoroughly, so two or three readings of the novel are advisable. However, make sure that your written responses do not simply retell the story. Use your knowledge of the novel to select the best quotations and references to explain the point you are making in your writing.

Chapters 19–22

Amir makes the journey back to Kabul, driven by Farid, a former Mujahideen (Islamist Afghan fighter), who cannot disguise his contempt for him. They stop overnight at Farid's brother's home, where Amir is struck and embarrassed by the family's generosity despite their poverty. Farid slowly warms to Amir once he knows why he is in Afghanistan and promises to help. Despite warnings, Amir is dumbfounded by the devastation he witnesses in Kabul.

They find the orphanage where Sohrab is. The director reluctantly reveals that he has been removed from the orphanage by a local Taliban leader who sexually abuses children. In a fit of rage, Farid attacks the director, who says that he had no choice as the Taliban are in control. He reveals where they can find the Taliban leader and hopefully the boy.

Amir visits his childhood home and is shocked by its dilapidated state, although the area has avoided the worst of the violence. He visits the pomegranate tree and sees the names he carved many years before.

The next day, he and Farid go to the local stadium where they are told the Taliban leader will be. They witness him stoning a man and woman to death during half-time at a football match and arrange to meet him the following day. The Taliban leader is revealed as none other than Assef, who raped Hassan as a boy. He delights in informing Amir of his role in the Taliban slaughter of innocent Hazara in Mazar-i-Sharif in 1998.

Sohrab is presented, dressed in traditional dress with bells on his feet and wearing make-up. He is made to dance and is being held as a child sex slave. Assef tells a stunned Amir that he must fight for Sohrab and orders his guards to leave them alone with only the boy present. He then proceeds to viciously batter Amir, who is no match for him. It is Sohrab who saves Amir by shooting Assef in the left eye with a marble fired from a slingshot he had hidden in his trousers. They flee the house and make their escape with Farid.

Activity 6

Write a paragraph explaining why it is necessary for the plot that Assef is the Taliban leader Amir must confront at the end of the novel.

Key quotations

"If I deny him one child, he takes ten. So I let him take one and leave the judging to Allah." *(Chapter 20)*

"You don't know the meaning of the word 'liberating' until you've done that, stood in a roomful of targets, let the bullets fly, free of guilt and remorse, knowing you are virtuous, good, and decent. Knowing you're doing God's work." *(Chapter 22)*

Chapters 23–25

Amir has extensive injuries that require serious medical attention. A traumatised Sohrab reveals that his father told him about Amir, but the boy is cautious and flinches at human contact. Rahim Khan writes to Amir, telling him that he has gone away to die and does not wish to be contacted. He has left Amir money and reveals that he knows about his cowardice in the alley when Hassan was attacked. He urges him to find reconciliation in all things.

The proposed foster family does not exist. Fearing that the hospital is no longer safe and that the Taliban are after him, Amir leaves for Islamabad with Sohrab.

On arrival, Amir says goodbye to Farid and pays him $2000. Having fallen asleep, he wakes to find that Sohrab has gone. He locates him at a mosque. An emotional Sohrab talks about the guilt and shame he feels as a result of the abuse he has suffered.

Amir explains that he and Hassan had the same father and the two hug. Amir states that he plans to adopt Sohrab and then promises to take him to America. Sohrab agrees. Amir visits the American Embassy in Islamabad where he is told he will not be able to adopt Sohrab and take him home, news which Sohrab takes very badly.

In the meantime, Soraya informs Amir that if he can get Sohrab into America first, they may be able to adopt him then. When he goes to tell Sohrab of this, he finds that he has attempted suicide. Amir rushes Sohrab to hospital where he prays for only the second time in his life. Sohrab survives but must be resuscitated twice.

Amir eventually gets Sohrab into America, where Soraya warmly welcomes him. 9/11 happens and Afghanistan is now a constant feature on the news and in the papers. Sohrab is mute, overwhelmed by the terrible events in his life. Amir admits that the weight of this hangs heavily over their home. However, during the 2002 Afghan New Year celebrations in the park, Amir flies a kite with Sohrab and detects a faint smile on the boy's face. This gives him hope as he chases down a fallen kite.

> **Key quotations**
>
> God will forgive… I hope you can do the same. Forgive your father if you can. Forgive me if you wish. But, most important, forgive yourself. *(Chapter 23)*
>
> Sohrab's silence […] was the silence of one who has taken cover in a dark place, curled up all the edges and tucked them under. *(Chapter 25)*

Activity 7

a) The plot of a literary text can traditionally be broken down into five stages, as shown on the diagram on page 13. Research what each stage involves.

b) Create a table identifying which parts of the plot of *The Kite Runner* fit into each stage. For example, for exposition, Amir relates how he received a telephone call from Rahim Khan in Pakistan asking him to visit. This triggers thoughts and reflections about his childhood in Kabul.

c) To what extent do you believe that *The Kite Runner* fits neatly into this structural model? Give reasons for your answer.

Activity 8

What main plots and **subplots** can you identify in the novel?

non-linear narrative a story that is not told chronologically and includes flashbacks and/or flash-forwards

subplot the secondary events or storylines that run parallel to the main plots, reflecting, underpinning and developing them

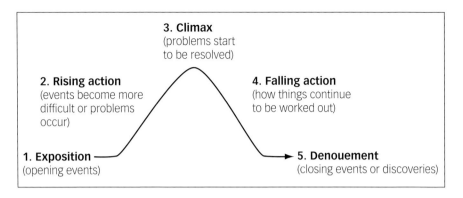

Structure

Structure refers to way in which the events of a plot are organised by the writer to maximise their impact on readers. It encompasses how time is organised and how the narrative voice, techniques and setting are used to tell the story.

How time is structured

Time is important in this novel and is constantly referred to. Real time covers the period from December 2001 to March 2002. However, chronologically, it covers a broader timeframe from Amir's birth in 1963, and even broader still given the reference to Baba's grandfather in 1915.

The Kite Runner has a **non-linear narrative** with a number of distinct periods. It is December 2001 in Chapter 1. This short first chapter acts as a framing device, establishing the importance of the past and its powerful impact on the present. From Chapter 2 until the end of Chapter 13, through an extended flashback, the period between the winter of 1963 up to approximately June 1991 is covered. During this section, earlier time references are present, such as Amir's grandfather hunting with King Nadir Shah in 1931. Chapter 14 is dated June 2001 and revisits the day Amir received Rahim Khan's phone call. It ends with the words, 'A week later, I sat on a window seat aboard a Pakistani International Airlines flight' *(Chapter 14)*, and this begins the period covered by Chapters 15–25, which culminates in the present, four days after 'a cool rainy day in March 2002' *(Chapter 25)*. During this timeframe, there are also many references to events from the past.

Hosseini deliberately organises time in this way, although it is potentially confusing for readers. Amir is tied to the past through his failure to intervene and help Hassan in the alleyway in 1975. This pivotal moment in his life becomes the pivotal moment for readers too. Hosseini's organisation of time helps achieve this, by making Amir present the events of his childhood from Chapter 2 until the rape scene in Chapter 7 in a largely chronological way.

Time then fractures during that moment through the inclusion of two memories and a dream recalled by Amir. The look on Hassan's face then triggers a third memory of the lamb sacrifice during past Eid al-Adha celebrations, the Islamic Festival of Sacrifice, which honours Ibrahim's willingness to sacrifice his son to Allah, through the sacrifice of a lamb.

This is not just a desperate child's attempt to distract himself from trauma. It represents how time and Amir's psychological development have shattered. Subsequently, his teenage and adult years, from Chapter 8 to the end of the book, are spent constantly looking back, reflecting and referencing the past, which weighs so heavily on his present. This creates a disjointed narrative, which reflects back on the event of the rape, just as the initial, linear narrative drives readers towards it.

Activity 9

a) Identify other occasions in the novel where the narrative is disrupted by a dream or a memory. What is the effect of each of these?

b) Write a paragraph explaining the **symbolic importance** of each of Amir's memories in Chapter 7.

The narrative voice

The retrospective, **first-person narration** of Amir is absolutely central to the success of *The Kite Runner*, a novel with the resolution of an individual's inner conflict at its heart.

Amir – the unreliable narrator

As this novel begins once all the events it contains are over and the conflicts have been resolved, Amir's narration presents readers with a dual perspective: he recalls events he experienced as a child, filtered through the lens of adulthood. The child Amir, for example, mistakenly believes that he killed his mother, something that adult Amir knows is not the case. As with all first-person narrations, issues of reliability exist. To what extent can readers believe that everything has been remembered accurately, given the traumatic events Amir experienced and the fact that they happened many years before? As he himself admits, 'time can be a greedy thing—sometimes it steals all the details for itself' *(Chapter 17)*.

Amir is also a limited narrator. He can only offer his interpretation of events, so subjectivity and bias may be present too. Does Amir's shame and guilt mean that he depicts himself more negatively and others more positively than was the case? This forces readers to be active participants, making judgements about the veracity and accuracy of Amir's accounts.

Narrative gaps also appear as the novel progresses. Other than one brief paragraph in Chapter 11, little detail is relayed about Amir and Baba's six months as refugees in Peshawar. Even less exists about the period between June 1991 and June 2001.

These narrative gaps can be seen in practical terms, as Hosseini focuses on time periods that link Afghanistan and Amir's national and personal histories. More significantly, however, they reinforce the sense that readers are excluded from specific and extended passages of time, contributing to the air of uncertainty and concerns about Amir's reliability as a narrator.

Activity 10

To what extent do you believe that Amir is a reliable narrator? Give reasons to support your answer.

Rahim Khan's stream of consciousness

Rahim Khan assumes the narration in Chapter 16. This fulfils an important function in the novel, filling in the narrative blanks in relation to Ali and Hassan as well as revealing the violence erupting after the Soviet invasion and the subsequent civil war. Although retrospective and first person, it is delivered as a **stream of consciousness**, a technique that offers a break from Amir's voice and allows Rahim Khan to speak uninterrupted. Amir, like readers, is a listener now. This permits Rahim Khan the space to cover a wide range of topics and time, moving seamlessly from one idea to another.

Hosseini uses sentence structure and punctuation to suggest the old man's thought processes and patterns of speech. For example, 'Now it was just me and the house and… I did my best' (Chapter 16). This is short and the use of ellipsis suggests a pause as Rahim Khan struggles to think of the words to suggest his feelings of disappointment that he could not maintain the house. Clearly, he feels that he let Baba down. Next, a dash is used to reflect his need to illustrate in detail for Amir just how bad his arthritis was: 'My knees and back were always aching— I would get up in the morning and it would take me at least an hour to shake the stiffness from my joints, especially in the wintertime' (Chapter 16). This reflects the unstructured, flexible way in which thought processes function. Rahim Khan's voice returns in his letter to Amir in Chapter 23.

Activity 11

Read from 'So one day' to '…mountains like jagged teeth' (Chapter 16). How does Hosseini try to reflect Rahim Khan's thought processes in this extract?

first-person narration the voice of a narrator who tells the story from their own point of view

stream of consciousness a narrative approach where the inner thoughts of an individual are communicated in a continuous flow

symbolic importance significant because of what things represent

Hassan's voice from the past

The third narrative voice is that of Hassan, presented through his letter to Amir in Chapter 17.

> ### Activity 12
>
> **a)** To what extent are Hassan's qualities as a child, as portrayed by Amir's narration, evident in the voice of Hassan's letter in Chapter 17?
>
> **b)** Why is it important to hear Hassan's voice at this stage of the novel?

Narrative techniques

Foreshadowing

Foreshadowing is when a writer hints at what is to come later. Hosseini uses this technique, especially at the very end of the earlier chapters. Chapter 1 concludes with: 'I thought of the life I had lived until the winter of 1975 came along and changed everything. And made me what I am today'. Immediately, readers are intrigued. He also uses it to warn that circumstances are about to change and not for the better, such as in Chapter 4, 'Because suddenly Afghanistan changed forever'. This creates dramatic tension and entices readers to read on to find out exactly what happens.

> ### Activity 13
>
> **a)** Find other examples of foreshadowing in Chapters 2–6. Explain what impact they have on readers.
>
> **b)** Why does Hosseini rely so heavily on the foreshadowing technique in the early chapters?

Motif

Motif refers to a recurring image or phrase that creates a pattern across a literary text. It is used to reintroduce key themes at opportune times for dramatic effect. This makes it an important structural feature.

A prominent motif in *The Kite Runner* is the pomegranate tree in the abandoned cemetery near Amir's house. The pomegranate has **symbolic** meaning in most major religions and is referenced in the Qur'an (the main holy book of Islam) as one of the fruits found in paradise. In the beginning, the tree holds positive associations of abundance, life and friendship. After Hassan's rape, Amir cannot bear to be near the tree and eventually it dies, symbolising the death of their friendship.

The pomegranate tree in the novel symbolises the best, and the death, of friendship

Activity 14

a) Other prominent motifs in the novel include kites, scars, ghosts, the lamb, the slingshot and illness. Track references to each of these and explain their symbolic importance.

b) Identify who says, **'For you, a thousand times over'** *(Chapter 1)* and when they say it. What is its significance on each occasion?

Parallels

Parallels work in association with many of the motifs in the novel. Given the novel's cyclical nature, these parallels contribute to the sense that Amir must go back in order to redeem himself and consequently move forward with his life. One very obvious parallel is how Hassan defends Amir by threatening Assef's left eye with his slingshot in Chapter 5. This is then echoed when his son Sohrab saves Amir from death at the hands of Assef in Chapter 22 by taking the very same left eye out with his slingshot.

Activity 15

What other parallels are there in the novel and what purpose do they serve?

Dreams and letters

Dreams and letters are flexible devices that can be inserted into the narrative to fulfil a number of functions. Dreams are used to foreshadow events, such as Hassan's dream about the monster in the lake in Chapter 7, or to reveal a character's psychological concerns, such as Amir's doubts and anxieties in relation to the same dream. Letters reinforce key themes and the relationship between characters, such as Rahim Khan's letter to Amir in Chapter 4; reintroduce characters, such as Hassan's letter to Amir in Chapter 17; or move the plot forward and provide psychological insight into another character, such as Rahim Khan's comments about Baba in his letter in Chapter 23.

Activity 16

Look carefully at the order of events in Chapter 17. Why does Hosseini place Hassan's letter to Amir near the beginning of this chapter?

symbolic something that represents something else, e.g. red roses are symbolic of love

Tips for assessment

Upgrade

A question that asks you to discuss a writer's authorial techniques or the way in which a writer shapes meaning requires you to comment on the structure of the novel. Even if you are not asked to comment on structure specifically, relevant knowledge can still be woven into your answer for other question types.

Activity 17

"Father says dreams always mean something." *(Chapter 7)*

Copy and complete the table below, identifying the dreamer, content and symbolic importance of each of the dreams listed. The first one has been done for you.

Content of dream and who has it	Symbolic significance of dream
Chapter 7 (dream 1) Hassan dreams of a lake that people claim has a monster at the bottom, so they are too afraid to go swimming. Amir ignores this claim and dives in, closely followed by Hassan. The people name the lake after the boys and charge people to use it.	• Hassan has a positive outlook about the challenges he faces. • Hassan's positivity is misplaced because danger does not always appear when you expect it. • Hassan believes in Amir and wants to help him overcome his anxiety about the kite tournament. • Hassan's realises that, like the monster, Amir has a cruel streak below his surface friendliness.
Chapter 7 (dream 2)	
Chapter 19	
Chapter 21	
Chapter 23	

Setting

Setting refers to where the action of the novel takes place and provides further structural cohesion. It contributes to our understanding of character, creates atmosphere and emphasises contrasts. In *The Kite Runner*, setting contributes significantly to the cyclical nature of the narrative, given how Amir's journey of **redemption** retraces his initial journey out of Kabul into the USA as a refugee.

redemption the action of saving, or being saved from, sin, error or evil

Kabul, Afghanistan

Kabul is the setting of both Amir's fall and his redemption. As a child, he enjoys a privileged existence growing up in the wealthy Wazir Akbar Khan district. The house built by his father is **'the most beautiful'** *(Chapter 2)* in the neighbourhood and Amir recalls its scale and opulence. There is also a clear sense of a more liberal Afghanistan at this stage.

Amir depicts a happy childhood too, with Hassan, playing childish pranks, flying kites, reading stories and visiting the cinema. During winter, the kite flying season, Amir is at his happiest and Kabul, to him, is at its best.

However, Amir does not live a carefree life: he blames himself for his mother's death during childbirth; he is increasingly aware of social and ethnic divides; he overhears his father speak of his disappointment in and estrangement from him.

Then Amir's world, as complex and confusing as it is, shatters further with the rape of Hassan. Suddenly, everything that was familiar and enjoyable is now the opposite. Amir cannot bear to be around Hassan, **'Because when he was around […] My chest tightened and I couldn't draw enough air'** *(Chapter 8)*. The admission **'And for the first time in my life, I couldn't wait for spring'** *(Chapter 8)* encapsulates his desire for things to move on and to leave winter and all that happened during it behind.

Activity 18

The rape of Hassan takes place in an alleyway. Why does Hosseini choose this setting?

Activity 19

Compare Amir's childhood home with the basement of the house in Jalalabad where he spends one week living as a refugee. What is the effect of the contrast?

Amir's return to Kabul as an adult is characterised by his shock at the destruction of the city following more than 20 years of war. He observes only **'Rubble and beggars'** *(Chapter 20)*, stares too long at the scowling Taliban on menacing patrol, and smells only the diesel, which has replaced the aromatic lamb kabob (spice lamb cooked on skewers) of his childhood. Kabul is now home to the powerless director of the orphanage, where children are at the mercy of depraved Taliban leaders, and football matches where men and women are stoned to death for breaking Shari'a law, which is based on teachings within Islam.

However, ultimately, Kabul is also the place where Amir must do what he did not do all those years before – fight. Before this climactic moment, Amir returns to his see his former home. While the area has escaped the worst of the damage, it is **'Like so much else in Kabul'**, a **'picture of fallen splendour'** *(Chapter 21)*. This visit, though, has an empowering effect on Amir, coming just before his showdown with Assef. Before leaving, he visits the pomegranate tree, now dead, where he runs his fingers over the names he carved all those years before. Amir's visit to Kabul is imbued with reflections and recollections, which intensify his resolve as he heads towards his destiny.

Tips for assessment

It is important to note that setting can be a room in a house or a sprawling city. For example, Kabul – before and after it is ravaged by war – is two distinct settings. However, within Kabul, there are numerous smaller settings such as the confines of Amir's home, his father's study, the hut in which Hassan is born, the cemetery with the pomegranate tree and the house where Assef lives as a Taliban leader.

Activity 20

Make a list of quotations and place them in two columns – one for positive descriptions of Kabul from Amir's childhood and the other for negative descriptions of Kabul when Amir returns as an adult.

Activity 21

a) Look again at the incident where Amir meets a former university lecturer now begging in the streets. What is the significance of this encounter?

b) What is significant about the fact that the Taliban leaders have taken up residence in the neighbourhood where Amir used to live?

Activity 22

a) Write two paragraphs analysing how the setting closely associated with the Hazara people, such as the village in the Bamiyan province of Hazarajat where Hassan and Farzana live, is depicted in the novel.

b) How does this contrast with the presentation of Kabul after the Taliban have taken over?

California, USA

Amir and Baba move to Fremont, California, in the early 1980s, a journey made by many Afghan refugees at the time, drawn to the climate, an open and diverse population, and also a generous welfare system. America is presented as a place where Amir is more at home than his father. Baba's proud nature means that he refuses lessons 'to improve his broken English' *(Chapter 11)* and his sense of honour sees him quick to secure employment to avoid state handouts. As an assistant at a petrol station, he worked hard – 'Six days a week, Baba pulled twelve-hour shifts' *(Chapter 11)*.

Key quotation

"I don't want to forget anymore," *(Chapter 21)*

This working-class existence is far removed from the quality of life Amir enjoyed in Afghanistan. Unsurprisingly, the different culture also creates problems for the older man, most noticeably at the convenience store, where Baba is indignant and aggressive when asked to produce identification to verify his cheque. Amir's diplomatic handling of the situation with the store owners, who are Vietnamese and obviously immigrants themselves, makes clear that the son is adjusting much more easily than the father, one and a half years after their arrival.

America is certainly a land of opportunity for Amir, but also 'Someplace with no ghosts, no memories, and no sins' *(Chapter 11)*. Having embraced it, he enjoys academic and professional success, graduating from high school then university, and becoming a published writer. In America, he also finds personal happiness in his wife Soraya, whom he meets at the San Jose flea market. The market becomes a home from home for Baba and the many other Afghan immigrants who 'were working an entire section' where 'Afghan music played in the aisles' *(Chapter 11)*. Such behaviour is unsurprising among immigrant communities seeking security. Such an environment, though, forces Amir to court Soraya according to strict Afghan custom.

As a setting, America is not without its pain for Amir either. It is here he loses Baba to cancer and has to accept he will never father a child. Ultimately, however, it is to America that Amir returns with Sohrab – his duty done, his past sins atoned for and his 'family' complete.

Activity 23

How does Hosseini suggest that life in the USA is not conducive to Baba, General Taheri and Khala Jamila?

Peshawar, Pakistan

Amir emerges from a dark, airless oil tanker onto Pakistan soil as an 18-year-old refugee with his father. His relief that Peshawar is now only a bus ride away is destroyed immediately when he witnesses the deaths of Kamal and his grief-stricken father. At the beginning of the next chapter, both Amir and Baba are in the USA with little further detail about Peshawar, despite spending six months there. Peshawar, however, returns to play a central role in the narrative. It is from here that Rahim Khan, having fled the conflict in Kabul, contacts Amir to request he visit, informing him of 'a way to be good again' *(Chapter 1)*.

It is also in Peshawar that Rahim Khan fills the narrative gaps, such as how the political conflict in Kabul developed, how and why Rahim Khan located Hassan, and how Hassan's life developed. On his return, Amir observes positively how **'The city was bursting with sounds'** *(Chapter 15)*, but the revelations that await him there are life-changing: Rahim Khan is dying and knows what happened in the alley all those years ago; Hassan and Farzana are dead; Rahim requests that Amir retrieve Sohrab from the orphanage; and finally the news that Baba fathered Hassan. All of this leaves Amir feeling bewildered and dumbfounded.

It is also in Peshawar that Amir ultimately makes the decision to go and get Sohrab, redeem himself and **'end the cycle'** *(Chapter 18)*. The next time he returns, Amir is recovering from Assef's beating. His former emotional heartbreak and anguish are now replaced by severe and extensive physical injuries, but finally Amir has acted like the man his father wanted him to be and, more importantly, his debt to Hassan is paid. This is evident in his dream while in the hospital, in which the man wrestling the bear is not Baba but Amir himself.

Activity 24

What other evidence is there in Chapter 23 that Amir has atoned for his past actions?

Islamabad, Pakistan

Islamabad is Pakistan's capital and home to the Faisal Mosque, the fourth largest mosque in the world. In Islamabad, Amir flees from the hospital to escape the Taliban and Sohrab runs away in Chapter 24 to the famous mosque. Sohrab also opens up about his abuse, Amir explains how he and Hassan are half-brothers, complications over the adoption arise, and Sohrab attempts suicide. Significantly, it is in Islamabad that Amir's religious awakening takes place.

> **Key quotation**
>
> Baba was wrong [...] There is a God, there has to be, and now I will pray... *(Chapter 25)*

Jalalabad, Afghanistan

Jalalabad is one of Afghanistan's five largest cities and an important trading and social hub. It appears first in Chapter 8 after Amir's success flying kites and the rape of Hassan. Amir, who has been feeling closer to Baba, suggests that they visit the cinema there so he can be alone with his father. However, Baba invites more than two dozen members of his extended family so the plan is thwarted. Things deteriorate further when Amir throws up in the truck, embarrassing Baba. On closing his eyes, he is tortured by a vision of **'Hassan's brown corduroy pants discarded on a pile of bricks in an alley'** *(Chapter 8)*.

At his aunt's house, an image of familial happiness and togetherness is depicted, from which Amir is completely removed. Although those present are **'still ranting** about the kite tournament' *(Chapter 8)*, Amir feels 'empty', despite finally having what he had 'wanted all those years' *(Chapter 8)*. That night he cannot sleep and speaks aloud his guilt: "I watched Hassan get raped" *(Chapter 8)*. Jalalabad offers no escape from his past deed. In fact, it is here that these feelings powerfully crystallise, with Amir believing that he is the monster at the bottom of the lake in Hassan's dream.

Five years later, aged 18, Amir returns. This time, however, he is a travel-sick refugee with Baba, fleeing the now Soviet-controlled Kabul. Tricked by the unscrupulous Karim, they spend a week in a rat-infested basement shared with 30 other Afghan refugees, one of whom is Kamal, who aided in the rape of Hassan. He is a shell of his former self, having been sexually assaulted himself by a group of men. The cramped and claustrophobic conditions clearly contrast with the luxurious lifestyle Baba and Amir have hastily left behind.

Amir's final return to Jalalabad is with Farid as a 38-year-old adult, where the city becomes a further staging post on his journey towards redemption. He is again travel sick, showing his continued immaturity and physical weakness. He notes a landscape transformed by violence and how, symbolically, the sweet scent of sugarcane, which previously permeated the city, can no longer be detected. Amir is treated with great respect by Farid's brother Walid, at the expense of his own children. Walid represents the traditional Afghan values of hospitality and respect, despite his impoverished status after years of war. That night Amir is haunted by a dream in which he is the Taliban soldier killing Hassan, although after this, he momentarily feels a reconnection to the land. As a setting, Jalalabad by turns disappoints, terrifies, haunts and humiliates Amir.

> **Key quotation**
>
> I understood the nature of my new curse: I was going to get away with it. *(Chapter 8)*

 Activity 25

How do the various men in Chapter 10 represent different aspects of Afghanistan?

Writing about structure

The structural features of a novel, such as where and how the action starts and how the story moves towards its resolution, will help you understand how the writer has shaped their narrative. Hosseini uses location and time particularly to reflect the emotional and physical turbulence his characters endure. These structural decisions are relevant in a number of different question types related to character and theme, so remember to consider how structure affects the whole of the story when faced with an exam question.

Biography of Khaled Hosseini

- 4 March 1965 – Khaled Hosseini was born in Kabul, Afghanistan, into an upper middle-class family.
- 1970–73 – His family lived in Tehran, Iran, due to his father's work as a diplomat with the Afghan Foreign Ministry.
- 1980 – His family sought political asylum in the USA, settling in San Jose, California. His mother, formerly vice-principal of a high school, became a waitress and his father a driving instructor; Hosseini spoke no English on arrival.
- 1988 – He graduated with a biology degree from Santa Clara University, California.
- 1989 – He studied medicine at the University of California.
- 1996 – He became a practising doctor.
- 2001 – Hosseini returned to Afghanistan for the first time since 1976, stating that 'he felt like a tourist in [his] own country'.

Khaled Hosseini emigrated to the USA as a 15-year-old in 1980

- 2003 – *The Kite Runner* was published.
- 2006 – Hosseini became a Goodwill Envoy for the United Nations.
- 2008 – The Khaled Hosseini Foundation, a non-profit organisation, was established in Afghanistan by Hosseini.

> ### Key quotations
>
> The end, the *official* end, would come first in April 1978 with the communist coup d'état, and then in December 1979, when Russian tanks would roll into the very same streets where Hassan and I played, bringing the death of the Afghanistan I knew and marking the start of a still ongoing era of bloodletting. *(Chapter 5)*
>
> "When the Taliban rolled in and kicked the Alliance out of Kabul, I actually danced on that street… People were so tired of the constant fighting…" *(Chapter 15)*
>
> Soon after the attacks, America bombed Afghanistan, the Northern Alliance moved in, and the Taliban scurried like rats into the caves. *(Chapter 25)*

Tips for assessment

Upgrade

Knowing about Hosseini's life and events during it is useful because they will inform and enrich your reading of the novel. However, in your responses you should not write at length about these. Where appropriate, a biographical reference that illustrates your understanding further or supports analysis is best.

Afghan history

Writers are influenced by the world around them and their novels are a product of the times in which they live. Amir's personal history in *The Kite Runner* is woven into the troubled and violent history of Afghanistan. As a result, there are many references to contemporary culture as well as historical, political and religious ones. Understanding these is very important in order to appreciate the novel fully. Afghanistan has two official languages: Dari and Pashto. However other languages, such as Uzbeki, Turkmani, Pachaie, Nuristani, Baluchi and Pamiri, are also spoken in some parts of the country.

Afghanistan

Afghanistan is located on the continent of Asia, has a population of more than 35 million people and is ranked the 41st largest country in the world by geographical area, according to the UN at time of publication. It is ethnically, religiously and linguistically diverse. Positioned at the centre of a number of important trade routes, Afghanistan is landlocked, sharing borders with Iran, Turkmenistan, China, Pakistan, Tajikistan and Uzbekistan. The borders with Iran and Pakistan have proved difficult to secure and monitor.

The three major land regions of Afghanistan are the dry and dusty northern plains, the central highlands and the deserts of the south-western lowlands. Two significant physical features are the Hindu Kush mountain range, which provides the country's highest peak, and the Khyber Pass, which connects it with Pakistan. The country's climate is characterised by extremes: summers are dry and very hot, while winters are cold with lots of snow. There is very little rainfall, a problem managed through irrigation from the country's rivers. On his re-entry to the country, driven by Farid, Amir notes, 'The arid, imposing mountains sat along deep gorges and soared to jagged peaks' *(Chapter 19)*. This vast, sprawling country remains one of the least developed in the world, with a low life expectancy, poor literacy levels and an economy ruined by war.

Afghanistan

The Kite Runner is a celebration of Afghanistan – its people, its culture, its traditions and its languages. References to these infuse the novel so readers are constantly learning about a country which they had most likely previously only associated with terrorism, violence and oppression. Everyday life is depicted. Hassan and Amir play the card game *panjpar*. *Dogh* (yoghurt drink) and *sabzi challow* (spinach stew with rice) are consumed. Farid wears the *pirhan-timban* (knee length shirt and trousers) and a *pakol* (soft round hat). Afghan wedding and funeral ceremonies are celebrated. In doing this, Hosseini challenges readers to reconsider their preconceptions of Afghanistan and also the validity of the West's view of the world and itself.

Activity 1

a) Research the following cultural references: *Ayena Masshaf, namaz, watan*.

b) Keep a log of other social and cultural references as you read the novel.

Activity 2

Look again at the description of the rituals involved during the Eid al-Adha celebration in Chapter 7.

a) What does this event reveal about Afghan culture?

b) What does it reveal about Baba?

c) How does it contribute to the theme of the father/son relationship?

Pashtun and Hazara

Pashtuns are an Eastern Iranian people. Although a significant minority group in Pakistan, they are the largest ethnic and most dominant group in Afghanistan and have been for hundreds of years. Most Pashtuns are Sunni Muslims, speak Pashto and follow the laws of Pashtunwali, a moral code governing all aspects of personal and community life. It emphasises:

- hospitality
- refuge to all guests seeking help
- swift revenge for wrongs inflicted
- the admission of guilt for wrongdoing.

Pashtuns have played a significant role in Afghanistan's history and still do so today.

The Pashtuns originated in the eastern parts of Iran and are now the dominant group in Afghanistan

The Hazaras are a minority people in Afghanistan, accounting for some 20% of the population. They are predominantly Shi'a Muslims of Mongol descent who speak Hazaragi, a Persian dialect. Due to their origin, the Hazara have an appearance that is distinctive from their fellow countrymen. Coupled with their religious differences, this has led to them being

The Hazaras are of Mongol descent and are discriminated against in Afghanistan

discriminated against by the majority Pashtun and persecuted by groups such as the Taliban, who deliberately targeted the Hazaras through ethnic cleansing. This hatred can be traced back to the casual **sectarianism** Amir hears: 'people called Hazaras *mice-eating, flat-nosed, load-carrying donkeys' (Chapter 2)*.

Activity 3

a) To what extent can you see the four codes of Pashtunwali listed on page 26 exemplified in the characters of Baba, Amir and Rahim Khan?

b) Find further references in the novel to the attitude of Pashtuns towards Hazaras, as well as the violence inflicted upon them.

Sunni and Shi'a Muslims

These are two groups of the same religion – Islam. Sunni Muslims constitute about 85% of all Muslims and are spread across the world, while Shi'a Muslims are in more concentrated areas across Iran, Iraq and Pakistan.

The major difference between the groups stems from the debate over who had the right to lead Islam following the Prophet Muhammad's death in 632 AD. Sunnis believe that their leader should be elected. Abu Bakr subsequently became the first leader or *caliph*. Shi'a Muslims believe that Muhammad's successor should have been one of his direct descendants and recognise this as Ali ibn Abi Talib, Muhammad's cousin and son-in-law. In essence, a political divide subsequently became a religious one. Although Sunni and Shi'a Muslims share the basic tenets of Islam, there are differences in terms of the rituals of prayer, celebration and commemoration.

sectarianism discrimination from religious intolerance

a) Research the Five Pillars of Sunni Islam and the Ten Obligatory Acts of Shi'a Islam. In what ways do the Sunni and Shi'a practices and beliefs differ?

b) Compare the attitudes to religion of Baba and Amir with those of Ali and Hassan. What does this suggest about their characters and how does it influence how you react to them?

Independence and the Monarchy (1921–1973)

During the 19th century, Britain sought to maintain the stability of its Indian empire and ward off the threat from Russia by controlling Afghanistan. This resulted in three Anglo–Afghan wars. In 1919, Amanullah Khan declared independence from Britain and, following the end of the third conflict in 1921, full independence was achieved. For three years, King Amanullah attempted a range of social reforms, which many considered too radical. He was ousted in 1929 by Habibullah Kalakani who, in turn, was assassinated and killed nine months later by Nadir Khan. In 1933, Khan was assassinated. Some idea of the status of Amir's family during Khan's rule can be seen in 'an old, grainy photo of my grandfather and King Nadir Shah taken in 1931' *(Chapter 2)*. Nadir Khan was succeeded by his son Mohammed Zahir Khan, who ruled over a peaceful and stable Afghanistan until a military coup in 1973 led by the prime minister and the king's cousin, Mohammed Daoud Khan.

The Republic (1973–1979)

Daoud Khan proclaimed Afghanistan a republic and himself president. His regime initially established closer links with the USSR, but Daoud later proposed more rights for women, tried to modernise the country and initiated a new foreign policy aimed at reducing Soviet and communist influence. This met with strong opposition from the People's Democratic Party of Afghanistan (PDPA) and the USSR. His rule ended in 1978 when he and his family were killed during the Saur Revolution led by the PDPA's Taraki, Amin and Karmal. Undermined by intense factional infighting and violent opposition to their anti-religious policies from the pro-Islam Mujahideen, the Soviet Army intervened in 1979 to bolster the new and failing Democratic Republic of Afghanistan, 'bringing the death of the Afghanistan I knew and marking the start of a still ongoing era of bloodletting' *(Chapter 5)*, according to Amir.

The Soviet–Afghan War (1979–1989)

What was initially envisaged as a six-month intervention became a ten-year conflict. The Soviet Army stormed Kabul and installed the more politically acceptable Karmal. Alongside the army of the Democratic Republic of Afghanistan, the Soviets fought against a range of groups who came together under the banner of the Mujahideen to fight for a state free of Soviet interference and governed by Islamic principles. With the USA subsequently intervening to back Mujahideen forces, this meant the war also became an indirect conflict between the USA and USSR, whose relationship had been tense ever since the end of the Second World War. In 1986, the Soviets replaced Karmal with Najibullah as president. However, the Mujahideen were incredibly determined and when the financial, military and political cost became too great, the Soviets withdrew in 1989. Najibullah ruled until 1992. An estimated two million civilians, 90,000 Mujahideen fighters and 15,500 Soviet soldiers were killed.

> **Activity 5**
>
> Write a paragraph, using carefully selected supporting quotations, analysing the portrayal of the Soviet Army in the novel.

The Mujahideen, the Islamic State of Afghanistan and Civil War (1992–2004)

The term 'mujahideen' is the plural form of 'mujahid' which means one who is fighting a 'holy war'. It is used to describe the disparate military factions that fought against President Taraki's Soviet-backed regime and then against the Soviet Army and the army of the Democratic Republic
of Afghanistan between 1979 and 1992. Although initially lacking organisation and a coherent strategy, the seven main Mujahideen groups united in 1985, calling themselves the Islamic Unity of Afghanistan Mujahideen. They drew support, in the form of weapons, intelligence and finance, from a number of countries including the USA, Saudi Arabia and Pakistan but also from sources right across the Muslim world, which supported their objective of an Islamic state in Afghanistan.

The Mujahideen proved itself to be a committed, effective, fierce enemy, playing a major role in driving the Soviets out of Afghanistan and later removing their puppet President Najibullah. This is illustrated in Amir's description of Farid: **'At fourteen, he and his father had joined the jihad against the *Shorawi*. They had fought in the Panjsher Valley for two years until helicopter gunfire had torn the older man to pieces'** *(Chapter 19)*.

With no common enemy, however, the Mujahideen descended into internal conflict as previous divisions resurfaced. Unable to provide stable government, the Islamic State of Afghanistan, as they had renamed the country, descended into civil war as former comrades fought each other over control of Kabul.

The Taliban and the Islamic Emirate of Afghanistan

From this violence and political instability the Taliban emerged in 1994. Its members were Pashtun students from eastern and southern Afghanistan who had been educated in traditional Islamic schools and had fought during the Soviet–Afghan War. The Taliban spread quickly across the fragmented country, seizing power from Mujahideen warlords, and proclaimed Afghanistan the Islamic Emirate of Afghanistan. By 1996, the Taliban had control of Kabul.

The Taliban became infamous for the barbaric way it enforced Islamic fundamentalist principles through Shari'a law. For this reason, many countries failed to recognise the Taliban as the official leaders of the country. Women, in particular, lost the most basic human rights. *The Kite Runner* depicts its shocking savagery as testimony to its occurrence. Ironically, Rahim Khan reveals that **'People were so tired of the constant fighting'** *(Chapter 15)* that the Taliban's entry into Kabul was welcomed. He depicts a people desperate for an end to bloodshed but unaware of its huge cost. Backed by Saudi Arabia and Pakistan, the Taliban governed roughly three quarters of Afghanistan at the height of its power, until the US-led invasion of the country following the 9/11 attacks. The Taliban subsequently regrouped in Pakistan and, despite losing their leader Mullah Omar, it still exists today, carrying out deadly attacks on its political and religious opponents.

> **Key quotation**
>
> "Peace at last. But at what price?" *(Chapter 15)*

The Northern Alliance

In 2001, the Northern Alliance controlled less than 10% of Afghanistan. It had been formed in the 1990s by members of the Mujahideen, formerly at the forefront of the former Islamic State of Afghanistan, to fight the Taliban. Working with the US-led coalition, which recognised it as the group officially leading the country, the Northern Alliance played a prominent role in pushing the Taliban out of power. With this defeat, the Alliance was dissolved and its members took up positions in the democratically elected government of Hamid Karzai in 2004. Despite their intention to drive the Taliban out, the Northern Alliance is heavily criticised by Rahim Khan. It is this force that destroys Baba's orphanage. He recalls in horror how "sifting through the rubble [...] There were body parts of children" *(Chapter 15)*. He also mentions one former Mujahideen leader specifically, signalling him out for criticism: "Gulbuddin and his cohorts firing on anything that moved" *(Chapter 15)*.

> **Key quotation**
>
> Rahim Khan told me how, when the Northern Alliance took over Kabul between 1992 and 1996, different factions claimed different parts of Kabul. *(Chapter 15)*

Al-Qaeda and 9/11

Al-Qaeda, meaning 'the Base', is a militant Sunni Islamist group founded in 1988 by former members of the Mujahideen, including Osama bin Laden. Basing itself in Afghanistan, the group enjoyed the support and protection of the Taliban, which enabled it to grow in numbers. Its radical aim was an end to all foreign influence in Muslim countries and the creation of a *caliphate*, a unified, purely Islamic state right across the Muslim world.

To this end, it carried out guerrilla attacks on both civilian and military targets across a number of countries. The most infamous of these was the 9/11 attack on the USA, which was the biggest ever terrorist attack on American soil and stunned the world. In total, 2996 people died. In its aftermath 'the world changed' *(Chapter 25)*, as Amir states, and the attack produced a ferocious backlash and crackdown by governments across the world on those suspected of terrorist activity. Once again, Afghanistan was in the eye of the storm when George W. Bush announced a 'war on terror'.

Activity 6

Find examples of Taliban oppression, particularly against women, in the novel. Use them to write an explanation of how Hosseini builds a realistic picture of fear and repression within the Afghanistan that Amir returns to.

The Western Coalition and the War on Terror

Having requested that the Taliban hand over Osama bin Laden for trial in the USA and having had that request refused, one month after 9/11 a US-led international coalition, including countries such as Britain and France, launched attacks on Al-Qaeda and the Taliban in Afghanistan. Their objectives were to capture or kill Osama bin Laden, destroy Al-Qaeda and remove the Taliban from power. In November, Kabul had been seized. By March 2002, the Taliban had been forced out of the mountainous areas in the east to which they had retreated. However, having regrouped in Pakistan, they were soon launching guerrilla-style revenge attacks.

Amir arrives back in the USA one month before the 9/11 attacks and comments on how 'Suddenly, people were standing in grocery store lines and talking about the cities of my childhood' *(Chapter 25)* as Afghanistan, bizarrely for an Afghan immigrant, flooded the consciousness of the American people through daily news broadcasts.

Immigration

Amir and his father are immigrants, just like the many other Afghan people who make their section of the San Jose flea market a home from home. It is a place where 'You greeted the guy across the aisle, you invited him for a bite of potato *bolani*, or a little *qabuli*, and you chatted. You offered *tassali*, condolences, for the death of a parent, congratulated the birth of children' *(Chapter 11)*.

Afghanistan has a history of movement among its people, especially since ethnic groups found themselves divided by the redrawing of borders following European empire building. Between 1979 and 1989, when the Soviets invaded, more than five million people fled, predominantly into Pakistan but also Iran, and 800,000 more moved within the country. A smaller number of refugees made their way to the USA at the time of the Soviet invasion and in succeeding years. There were an estimated 45,000–75,000 living in the USA by the time the Soviets left in 1989. The subsequent civil war and ensuing international conflict saw further waves of migration, as people escaped the cycles of political change and the accompanying violence. Consequently, Afghans are currently one of the largest refugee populations in the world.

Sport

> ### Activity 7
>
> Why do you think Hosseini places Amir back in the USA at the time of the 9/11 attacks?

Buzkashi, meaning 'goat pulling', is the Afghan national sport. Amir explains the rules of the game in Chapter 3 and calls it the **'national passion'**. Buzkashi is considered one of the most dangerous sports in the world – for both player and spectator – and fatalities are not uncommon. The game has its origins in goat and cattle rustling, in which the owners would try to prevent thieves on horseback from stealing their animals. In its apparent lawlessness, it is said to reflect the violent power struggles that the country has endured for centuries. Amir's chance to

Buzkashi is the national sport of Afghanistan

bond with his father at a Buzkashi tournament fails when the brutal death of one of the riders leaves him in tears. On the way home, he recalls **'Baba's valiant efforts to conceal the disgusted look on his face as he drove in silence'** *(Chapter 3)*. Buzkashi was banned by the Taliban.

Kite fighting

Kite fighting has a long history in Afghanistan, although practised in other countries too. In Chapter 6, Hosseini describes the culture surrounding kite fighting in great detail and again, in Chapter 8, allows Amir to describe, in commentary fashion, the aerial fight in the tournament. This reveals Amir's passion for kite fighting but also celebrates a powerful force in Afghan culture, for kite flying still unites young and old, rich and poor, upper and lower class in Afghanistan. Given that kite flying was banned by the Taliban, Hosseini clearly asserts the importance of this activity to the people of his homeland and also very publically defies the Taliban ideologues through his choice of title for his novel. Interestingly, for a boy who is **"not violent"** *(Chapter 3)*, according to Rahim Khan, Amir is able to 'kill' his opponents' kites and also suffer the cuts caused to his fingers by the glass-encrusted string. On the day of the tournament, he wins despite the fact that his **'legs ached'** and his **'neck was stiff'** *(Chapter 7)*.

Amir remarks how 'The rules were simple: No rules' *(Chapter 6)*, again reflecting the Afghans' fierce independence of mind. The sport says much about Afghan culture in that an activity that can be solitary, peaceful and enjoyed by both participant and observer suddenly becomes transformed into a battle of life or death. Amir comments how the kites fill the skies 'like paper sharks roaming for prey' *(Chapter 7)*.

Kite flying still unites the people of Afghanistan

Key quotations

Baba and I lived in the same house, but in different spheres of existence. Kites were the one paper-thin slice of intersection between those spheres. *(Chapter 6)*

Every winter, districts in Kabul held a kite-fighting tournament. And if you were a boy living in Kabul, the day of the tournament was undeniably the highlight of the cold season. *(Chapter 6)*

Activity 8

Explain the positive and negative associations of kites for Amir.

Soccer

Soccer, an imported sport, was first played in Afghanistan back in the early 1920s among high-school students in Kabul, who were introduced to it through foreign coaches. Its modest development was slow; by 1941, there were only two official teams in the capital. The first national team appeared in the same year, but its development and progress since has been hindered by years of conflict. Soccer, for Baba, 'was something to be passionate about' as 'real boys—played soccer' *(Chapter 3)*. It becomes a vehicle through which Baba attempts to mould his son into the type of person he wants him to be. Unfortunately, it has the reverse effect, for Amir 'hadn't inherited a shred of his athletic talents' *(Chapter 3)*. It is ironic that the Taliban continued to permit football while in power, despite it being an imported western sport.

Literature

The act of reading is present throughout the novel. Aged 11, Amir can recite swathes of verse, emerging victorious in a "Battle of the Poems" in which he 'took on the whole class and won' *(Chapter 3)*.

Amir references the poets Khayyám, Hãfez and Rumi. The latter's *Masnawi* consists of six books of poetry amounting to some 50,000 lines and outlines how those who believe and practise Islamic mysticism can find true love in God. Amir recounts how he **'read everything'** *(Chapter 3)*, citing native but also western authors such as Victor Hugo, Jules Verne, Mark Twain and Ian Fleming. These names suggest an eclectic mix, displaying an appreciation of great Persian literary figures as well as an enjoyment of adventure and daring action by European and American writers.

Literature plays an important role in the relationship between Amir and Hassan too. Amir reads **'poems and stories, sometimes riddles'** as well as the humorous **'misadventures of [...] Mullah Nasruddin'** *(Chapter 4)*. These were popular tales told by a wise fool, so called because in his stupidity he provides instruction. Another key book in the novel is the *Shahnameh*, the world's longest epic poem and the national epic poem of Greater Iran, written by the Persian poet Ferdowsi (between c. 977 and 1010 CE), about the mythical and historical past or Iran. The boys share the same favourite story from the poem, **"Rostam and Sohrab"** *(Chapter 4)*.

Key quotations

That was how I escaped my father's aloofness, in my dead mother's books. *(Chapter 3)*

I started spending my allowance on books. I bought one a week from the bookstore... *(Chapter 3)*

Hassan absently plucked blades of grass from the ground as I read him stories he couldn't read for himself. *(Chapter 4)*

Activity 9

a) Find and read the story of 'Rostam and Sohrab'. Does it have the same meaning for both Amir and Hassan? Explain your answer.

b) What parallels exist between this story and the father/son relationships in the novel?

Activity 10

What is the attraction for Amir and Hassan in the western movies they enjoy, such as *Rio Bravo* and *The Magnificent Seven*?

Activity 11

a) Read the three extracts opposite, which come from responses to a question asking students to comment on the relationship between Amir and Hassan in the novel. Which extract best demonstrates a good understanding of the text and incorporates an understanding of context? Rank all three, explaining your choices.

b) Rewrite and improve the answer you feel is weakest.

Extract 1

One major difference between the boys is that Amir is Pashtun and Hassan is Hazara. The Pashtuns originated in eastern Iran and are found in both Pakistan and Afghanistan, where they form the ethnic majority. They speak Pashto and are Sunni Muslims, who believe that the leader of Islam does not have to descend directly from the Prophet's family. The Hazara are of Mongolian descent. They speak Hazaraghi and are from the Shi'a branch of Islam. Throughout the 20th century, the Hazara have been subjected to severe social, economic and political discrimination. This being so, Amir has a much more privileged position in society than Hassan.

Extract 2

The boys have different ethnic and religious backgrounds, which accounts for their very different positions in society. Amir, being Pashtun and Sunni, holds a privileged position while Hassan, Hazara and Shi'a, is of lower status and comes from a minority community that faces discrimination and persecution. Such religious and ethnic divisions are deep-rooted 'Because history isn't easy to overcome', so Amir recognises the special quality and closeness of their bond, 'Hassan and I fed from the same breasts', but equally he acknowledges that he 'never thought of Hassan and me as friends' and that the gulf between them is unbridgeable and 'nothing was ever going to change that'.

Extract 3

Amir's privileged position stems from the fact that he is Pashtun and Sunni while Hassan, being Hazara and Shi'a, is destined to live with his father 'in a modest little mud hut', which directly contrasts with the opulence of Amir's home. Despite being good friends and enjoying each other's company, 'Sometimes, my entire childhood seems like one long lazy summer day with Hassan', Amir is well aware of how the social, religious and ethnic differences between them mean 'That Hassan would grow up illiterate' and that his fate 'had been decided the minute he had been born'.

Writing about context

It is important that you demonstrate a clear understanding of how *The Kite Runner* reflects social, cultural and historical contexts. Long passages describing Taliban rule, what life was like before the Soviet invasion or Afghanistan's history of immigration are not what the examiner is looking for. Your primary focus must be the text, but use your understanding of what was happening at the time to demonstrate your knowledge that the book is influenced and shaped by the specific era in which it is set.

Literary genres have essential characteristics that define them, but writers manipulate these, adapting and developing them, using them to their advantage, emphasising some characteristics and minimising others as their needs and intentions require. In this sense, a literary text can be part of more than one genre and subgenres can also appear.

The Kite Runner possesses the characteristics of a number of genres. First and foremost, it is a work of literary fiction, meaning that it was written with artistic intention and designed to entertain but also to challenge and instruct.

Fable

Fables are short stories designed to teach a moral lesson. They use non-human creatures such as animals and imbue them with human characteristics so that they can interact to reveal important lessons about life and emphasise the difference between right and wrong. Fables have existed for a very long time, passed down through the oral traditions of folklore, and are found in the literature of most cultures. Although initially targeted at adults with religious, political and social concerns, they later became used to educate children.

The most famous fables are those of Aesop, a storyteller and slave who lived in ancient Greece between 620 and 564 BC. *The Lion, the Witch and the Wardrobe* by C. S. Lewis is a good example of a novel that is a fable. Many critics have identified *The Kite Runner* as a fable too, despite the fact that it does not contain **anthropomorphised** creatures.

> ### Activity 1
>
> **a)** To what extent do you believe that *The Kite Runner* is a fable? Give reasons to support your view.
>
> **b)** Read a selection of Aesop's fables such as 'How Love and Peace Came to the Forest', 'Androcles and the Lion' and 'The Rat and the Elephant'. Which of these relate to the characters and themes in *The Kite Runner* and how?

Allegory

Linked closely to the idea of fable is **allegory**. Allegorical texts use a person, setting or event as a powerful **metaphor**, extended right across a text, to convey important, complex ideas about the themes and issues they are addressing. *Animal Farm* by George Orwell exemplifies this use of fable and allegory. The main protagonists are animals on a farm and their experiences are used to reflect events leading up to the Russian Revolution of 1917 and the Stalinist era of the Soviet Union.

Hosseini declared that the rape of Hassan in the alleyway is allegorical – he intended this brutal act to represent something beyond the physical act perpetrated by one boy on another.

Activity 2

a) In seeing the rape as allegorical, who or what could Hassan, Assef and Amir represent?

b) Some critics interpret the character of Amir as allegorical of the country of Afghanistan. Give reasons to support or contradict this reading of the novel.

c) In what other ways can the novel be seen to be allegorical?

Autobiographical fiction

This is a subgenre of autobiography and involves a writer drawing on some of their past experiences but presenting these ultimately as a work of fiction. Most characters and significant aspects of the plot of *The Kite Runner* are clearly made up but, equally so, some events reference or are inspired by Afghanistan's history as well as Hosseini's personal past. This allows the writer to develop real-life experiences, by exaggerating them for dramatic purpose. The writer can also take aspects of real people, and merge and exploit different features of their appearance and personality, to create

Sohrab finds it extremely difficult to engage with his new life in America after all his experiences in his home country

an entirely fictitious character who can then drive the plot, develop a theme or represent an important issue. Such texts possess grains of truth, which are woven into a fictitious framework. For example, Hosseini, like Amir, fled Kabul for the USA, so he has an appreciation of how difficult it is to assimilate into a foreign country and he understands what challenges the immigrant faces. However, he did not experience the trauma of watching a grown man shoot himself in the head, as Amir does.

 The setting in 1970s Kabul, the house where Amir lived, the films that he watches, of course the kite flying, the love of storytelling – all of that is from my childhood. The storyline is fictional.

(Khaled Hosseini, 'The "Kite Runner" Controversy', *Salon*, 9 Dec. 2007)

allegory a story, poem or painting in which the characters and events are symbols of something else, often political, religious or moral

anthropomorphised when non-human creatures are given human attributes

metaphor a direct comparison in which one thing is said to be another

Bildungsroman

Bildungsroman means a novel of education. The first work of this genre was *Wilhelm Meister's Apprenticeship* by Johann Wolfgang Goethe, published around 1795. Such narratives involve a central, young protagonist who is alienated from society and portrayed as immature and lacking worldly knowledge. The protagonist undertakes a challenging journey during which they develop psychologically and morally, and consequently mature. At the end of this process, they are able to function in and contribute positively to society. The genre quickly became popular and remains so today, and has become known as the 'coming of age' story. Charles Dickens's *Great Expectations* is a classic example of a Bildungsroman.

Activity 3

Below is a list of the conventions of the Bildungsroman genre. To help evaluate the extent to which the novel is a Bildungsroman, explain whether you think each one is present in *The Kite Runner* and find an example for those that are.

- The main protagonist is foolish or immature at the beginning.
- This character feels alienated from society and its values.
- There is an incident, such as a terrible loss, that triggers the protagonist's journey.
- There is a physical journey or a search for meaning by the main protagonist.
- The journey will be a difficult one that tests the main protagonist to their limits.
- An epiphany, or moment of revelation, occurs that is pivotal to the main protagonist's success.
- The main protagonist achieves growth and maturity.
- The main protagonist assimilates back into society.
- The future remains unclear at the end for the main protagonist, but they are better equipped to deal with the challenges of life.

The redemption story

This genre is linked to the Bildungsroman. The idea of redemption – salvation (being saved) from past sins and failures – comes from religious teachings but is a power-ful theme in all forms of literature. Examples include *Les Miserables* by Victor Hugo (1862) and *Tess of the d'Urbervilles* by Thomas Hardy (1891).

Amir is a flawed character even before the rape by Assef – full of petty jealousy when he watches Baba's moments of kindness towards Hassan. His failure to act during the attack, his subsequent framing of the innocent servant boy and its dire consequences all become the burden he cannot escape and for which he must atone. Hosseini recognises the redemption story genre in the opening chapter when Amir says, 'I knew it wasn't just Rahim Khan on the line. It was my past of unatoned sins' *(Chapter 1)*.

Activity 4

Dan McAdams, an American psychologist, argues that redemption is an intrinsically American concern. He identifies five stages to the **redemption arc**.

Copy and complete the table below, identifying the extent to which you believe *The Kite Runner* fits into McAdams's five stages. The first one has been done.

Stage	Meaning	Evident in *The Kite Runner*
1. Early advantage	The main protagonist is aware of their special status.	Amir is fully aware of his privileged position as a Pashtun Sunni in relation to Ali and Hassan.
2. Sensitivity to suffering	The main protagonist becomes aware of the unfairness of the world.	
3. Moral steadfastness	The main protagonist has a strong sense of right and wrong.	
4. Redemption sequences	A significant mistake becomes a means to achieve forgiveness for the main protagonist.	
5. Delivering from suffering and enhanced status	The protagonist commits to try to help others.	

Key quotations

There is a way to be good again. (Chapter 1)

A way to end the cycle. With a little boy. An orphan. Hassan's son. Somewhere in Kabul. *(Chapter 18)*

The novel and realism

As a novel, *The Kite Runner* is part of a literary tradition that can be traced back to the work of Daniel Defoe, author of *Robinson Crusoe* (1719). The characteristics of this work – its **epistolary** nature and **confessional** tone, the desire to instruct and the **autobiographical** narration – are all clearly evident in Hosseini's work. Subgenres of the novel soon followed.

autobiographical about the writer's own life and experiences

confessional revealing private thoughts or events that have happened that might be considered shameful or a secret

epistolary written in letters

redemption arc the journey of a character from bad to good

One of these, **literary realism**, started in the mid-19th century, lasting until the late 19th/early 20th century. Realism was a reaction to **Romanticism**, which prioritised emotion, the individual and the power of the imagination and nature. Realism, on the other hand, wanted to present the 'objective reality' of everyday life. Its writers wanted to portray the ordinary and everyday as honestly and accurately as possible, achieving a truthful and genuine representation of the real world. Classic European examples of the genre include Leo Tolstoy's *War and Peace* (1869) and Gustave Flaubert's *Madame Bovary* (1857). American writers of the genre include Henry James (1843–1916) and Mark Twain (1835–1910). Realist texts assume the quality of something like a historical document in how they chronicle the essence of a specific social group – usually the middle class. Aspects of *The Kite Runner* can be considered realist.

Activity 5

Read the conventions below, traditionally found in literary realism. Decide whether each one applies to *The Kite Runner* and explain your choices.

- Realist writers usually employ the novel form.
- Characters face difficult ethical decisions.
- A rising middle class is featured.
- Action and events are not sensationalised.
- Society, rather than the individual, is scrutinised.
- An **omniscient** narrator is usually employed.
- Class issues feature prominently.
- Lengthy passages describe everyday activities.
- Urban rather than rural settings are used.
- Straightforward language is employed to reflect the ordinary.
- Settings are recognisable and familiar.
- A critique of society is offered.
- Realist novels are usually long – more than 500 pages.

literary realism a movement in literature and art to present familiar things as they really are

omniscient all-knowing

Romanticism a movement in literature and art that celebrated imagination, emotion and the natural world

Epistolary novel

Deriving its name from the Greek word *epistle*, meaning a letter, 'epistolary' refers to novels written in the form of letters or documents such as diary entries, journals and newspaper clippings. The genre dates as far back as the 15th century and Diego de San Pedro's *Prison of Love*. The form became more widespread in the 18th century through the work of Samuel Richardson and his novels *Pamela* (1740) and *Clarissa* (1748). This approach allows

Letters are highly significant in the novel

readers to gain a better insight into the thinking and emotions of the protagonist. In novels involving more than one letter writer or contributor, it offers multiple perspectives. The narrative approach and the inclusion of letters in *The Kite Runner* is a nod towards this genre.

Activity 6

Explain the narrative function that Rahim Khan's letters perform.

Novel of manners

This is a subgenre of literary realism, so called because it focuses attention on a specific group within society and how they communicate, behave and interact – between themselves and with other social groups. This in turn reveals their values and thinking. In focusing on detailed observations of one social group, the writer is able to establish the moral code by which they live and judge others. How far others demonstrate the same values as this group will determine their acceptance into, or rejection by, the group. Jane Austen and Edith Wharton's novels are good examples of this subgenre; Austen's detailing the lives of rural, high-class English society in the early 19th century and Wharton's those of the privileged, urban American classes almost one hundred years later.

The nature of Hosseini's narrative draws attention to a specific stratum of Afghan society. He primarily depicts the life of the wealthy, middle-class Pashtun Sunnis in Kabul through Amir and Baba. As a result, readers are introduced to the world of the Hazara Shi'a servant class, as presented by Hassan and Ali. Following their flight to America, Hosseini again depicts, in some detail, the life of the formerly middle-class Pashtun Sunnis. This time they are foreigners, greatly reduced in status, living in a strange land, striving to make a life for themselves. Readers are again presented with how they interact, not only with Americans and other immigrants, but with each other in this new context.

Key quotations

While I ate and complained about homework, Hassan made my bed, polished my shoes, ironed my outfit for the day, packed my books and pencils. *(Chapter 4)*

Me a *mojarad*, a single young man, and she an unwed young woman. One with a *history*, no less. This was teetering dangerously on the verge of gossip material, and the best kind of it. *(Chapter 12)*

"Please think, Amir jan. It was a shameful situation. People would talk. All that a man had back then, all that he was, was his honor, his name, and if people talked… We couldn't tell anyone, surely you can see that." *(Chapter 17)*

Modernism and postmodernism

Modernism covers the period from the late 19th century to the early 20th century. As an artistic movement it was a reaction to realism, rejecting its rational understanding of the world and its emphasis on science.

After the First World War, and faced with the harsh realities of an unfamiliar and quickly developing urban world, growing numbers of modernist writers sought to reflect their uncertainty and fears in a new form of literature that experimented with accepted conventions. Consequently, they wrote about more condensed periods of time and focused on the internal conflicts of the individual through a first-person, non-linear narrative, with some using the stream of consciousness technique. Their narrators were unreliable and projected an alienation from the world around them in works that were deeply conscious of how they told the story and explicitly drew attention to that, rather than simply telling it. Many references and **allusions** were woven into their narrative as well.

James Joyce's *Ulysses* (1922) is considered a classic of the genre. It uses the stream of consciousness narrative technique to describe the ordinary events in a day in the life of main protagonists Stephen Dedalus and Leopold Bloom. Its length, narrative approach, rich use of allusion and a structure that mirrors Homer's epic poem *The Odyssey* creates a chaotic and disorientating feel. This is designed to reflect the complexity of contemporary life.

The Kite Runner, published in 2003, falls under the banner of **postmodernism**, which refers to the period after the Second World War until the present time. Postmodernism is obviously an outworking of modernism. The two concepts share similar characteristics such as the unreliable narrator, the fracturing of time and the conscious emphasis on the act of writing. However, they differ in a number of ways. For example, postmodernist texts reject outright meaning, instead promoting the idea of a lack of meaning or multiple meanings. This reflects the impossibility of one governing interpretation.

Postmodernist texts employ a simpler language, focus on external rather than internal worlds, and celebrate **high** and **low cultures**. Tellingly, they also challenge western values and the dominant western reading and representations of things.

> **Activity 7**
>
> Consider how far *The Kite Runner* fulfils the conventions of a postmodern text. Support your ideas with quotations and explanations.

War novel

Violent conflict has been present throughout history, so it is not surprising that writers have addressed this through writing in all its forms. The war novel is one that has the battlefield as its setting or characters whose primary worries and concerns are war. Its origins are found in the **epic poetry** of earlier periods, including Homer's *The Iliad*, Virgil's *The Aeneid* and the Old English saga *Beowulf*. Famous war novels include Leo Tolstoy's *War and Peace* (1869) about the Napoleonic Wars in Russia, Erich Maria Remarque's *All Quiet on the Western Front* (1929) about the experiences of German soldiers on the frontline during the First World War, and Joseph Heller's *Catch-22* (1961), a satirical view of the Second World War from an American perspective.

Conflict and war are omnipresent in *The Kite Runner*. At one end of the spectrum is the 'bloodless coup' *(Chapter 5)* of Daoud Khan in 1973 and at the other is the sickening barbarism of the Taliban. Hosseini also reflects a more recent reality – that of watching war from the safety of a living room via worldwide media using new technologies. Just as wars and how they are fought have changed, Hosseini, as an Afghan immigrant in America writing about his birthplace, is also part of a literary tradition, writing about war in a new way and posing new questions of his reader.

allusion a brief reference, which might be social, cultural, literary, political or historical

epic poetry long narrative poems set in the past and involving heroic characters and supernatural forces or gods

high culture referring to art forms, such as classical music, enjoyed by highly educated people

low culture referring to popular art forms, such as pop music, enjoyed by ordinary people

modernism a movement away from traditional forms or ideas, reconsidering what is meant by realism and influenced by psychological ideas

postmodernism a concept in art and literature that developed against modernism, distrusting theories and systems of ideas

Activity 8

a) How does Hosseini portray war as a loss of innocence? Use two or three carefully selected quotations to support your views.

b) Do you think that Hosseini portrays the Afghan people as having become desensitised to violence? Explain your ideas.

c) Explain whether you think the novel is narrated from an Afghan or an American perspective.

Confessional novel

Confessional novels are either real or fictitious works of autobiography in which the main protagonist offers up honest reflections on their failings. The first example of the genre was *The Confessions of St Augustine* (c. 397–400 AD), a spiritual examination of Saint Augustine of Hippo's transition from sinful youth to committed Christian. Another work, *Confessions of an English Opium-Eater* (1822), focused on Thomas de Quincey's drug addiction. While the former is almost philosophical in its nature, the latter offers a voyeuristic insight into a dark world. Both offer readers an intimate relationship with the individual who is 'confessing' what they have done and their innermost secrets and fears.

Key quotations

I already hated all the kids he was building the orphanage for; sometimes I wished they'd all died along with their parents. *(Chapter 3)*

Maybe Hassan was the price I had to pay, the lamb I had to slay, to win Baba. Was it a fair price? The answer floated to my conscious mind before I could thwart it: He was just a Hazara, wasn't he? *(Chapter 7)*

Activity 9

In what ways is Hosseini 'confessing' as much as Amir?

Historical fiction

Historical fiction reconstructs the past, incorporating real events or real people, or both, into a fictitious narrative. Well-known examples include *The Three Musketeers* (1844) by Alexandre Dumas and *A Tale of Two Cities* (1859) by Charles Dickens. Although it is generally believed that historical fiction requires a distance of some 60 years at least between events taking place and their being written about, it is impossible to say that *The Kite Runner* does not contain elements of this genre. Hosseini clearly documents the political, cultural and social systems of Afghanistan in a period covering Amir's birth in 1963 until 2002.

In this type of fiction, Hosseini's artistic licence is restricted if he is to reflect the history of the time accurately. This is achieved not simply through the veracity of factual things like dates, events and individuals' names; his characters, although fictional, must reflect the world and era being revisited through their behaviour, dress, opinions and values. Within this framework, Hosseini reflects specific periods of Afghanistan's history, but also encourages readers to think differently about the country's present and its people, having learned about its past.

Activity 10

'*The Kite Runner* makes clear that neither the individual nor the nation can escape history.'

To what extent do you agree with this statement? Give reasons for your answer.

Tragedy

At the end of Chapter 2, Amir reflects on his and Hassan's first words as children, saying, '**Looking back on it now, I think the foundation for what happened in the winter of 1975—and all that followed—was already laid in those first words.**' The feeling that these events were destined to happen and were unavoidable suggests that the novel draws on the conventions of the genre known as *tragedy*. This refers, originally, to a type of play first performed in ancient Greece with a strict set of conventions, for example Sophocles's *Oedipus Rex*, which was first performed around 429 BC. Shakespeare (1564–1616) is famous for his tragedies, such as *King Lear*, *Othello* and *Hamlet*. Over time, the term has become used to discuss other forms of literature, not just plays.

Activity 11

Research the conventions of tragedy. Write two or three paragraphs explaining if you think *The Kite Runner* can be considered a work of tragedy.

Writing about genre

It is important that you know how *The Kite Runner* contains elements of several genres and is not easily placed into just one category. Consider which genre you feel the novel most neatly fits into and practise writing a response about this as part of your revision. If you think Hosseini has challenged the conventions of that genre, explain how and why you think he has done so. What is the result?

Relating the novel to genres will help you get away from simply writing about the events of the story or the actions of the characters. It will enable you to consider the novel in a wider literary context and bring a sharper focus to your points.

Characterisation and Roles

Characters are deliberate constructs that allow a writer to introduce and explore a range of themes, reflect contextual issues, and convey different points of view and contrasting values.

Major characters

Amir

Amir is the novel's main protagonist and narrator. His formative years reflect a life of privilege as a member of the dominant Pashtun Sunni ethnic group, living comfortably in an affluent suburb of Kabul. In an Afghanistan that is politically stable and free of violence, he is portrayed as blessed, at least on the surface. Amir enjoys the generosity of a wealthy father, and has a servant boy to prepare his breakfast and always accept the blame when their childish pranks go wrong. He avoids corporal punishment in school because his **'father was rich and everyone knew him'** *(Chapter 8)*. It is no coincidence that 'Amir' translates as 'prince'.

However, the reality is very different. Amir is beset by huge emotional and psychological issues relating to his family. He misses his mother, who died giving birth to him. More potently, however, he feels responsible for her death. This dark guilt underlies his complex and difficult relationship with his father. Amir's estrangement from Baba is deep and profound: **'the truth of it was, I always felt like Baba hated me a little'** *(Chapter 3)*. He is acutely aware of the differences between them in terms of personality and qualities. Amir shows little sporting ability and displays physical 'weaknesses' such as car sickness. This is compounded when Amir actually hears his father express his shame aloud, **"If I hadn't seen the doctor pull him out of my wife with my own eyes, I'd never believe he's my son"** *(Chapter 3)*. Refuge from this reality is found in his mother's books and her love of the written word. Unfortunately, in fleeing one painful truth Amir is faced with the other: **'That was how I escaped my father's aloofness, in my dead mother's books'** *(Chapter 3)*.

Activity 1

Does it matter that there is no physical description of Amir until after his beating by Assef? Why do you think Hosseini chose to do this?

Key quotations

...the way I ached for the mother I had never met? *(Chapter 2)*

After all, I *had* killed his [Baba's] beloved wife... *(Chapter 3)*

But I hadn't turned out like him. Not at all. *(Chapter 3)*

Viewed from the outside, Amir and Hassan are presented as good friends who are very happy in each other's company. They involve themselves in the stereotypical activities and mischievous behaviour of young boys. Amir states fondly, 'Sometimes, my entire childhood seems like one long lazy summer day with Hassan, chasing each other between tangles of trees in my father's yard, playing hide-and-seek, cops and robbers, cowboys and Indians, insect torture' *(Chapter 4)*. Their relationship is reinforced further through two activities: reading and kite fighting.

Despite having described what was clearly a friendship, Amir says, 'The curious thing was, I never thought of Hassan and me as friends either. Not in the usual sense, anyhow' *(Chapter 4)*. This can be partly explained by the master/servant relationship in play within the home, and furthermore by the ethnic and religious divisions within the country, which both boys are very much aware of. At this point, Amir is awash with contradictions in trying to understand and explain his relationship with Hassan. On the one hand he states, 'I was a Pashtun and he was a Hazara, I was Sunni and he was Shi'a, and nothing was ever going to change that. Nothing' *(Chapter 4)*. Although, shortly afterwards he comments, 'But we were kids who had learned to crawl together, and no history, ethnicity, society, or religion was going to change that either' *(Chapter 4)*. Clearly, Amir's processing of the relationships in his life during his formative years is complex and problematical.

Such contradictions manifest themselves in contradictory behaviours. Amir can demonstrate the qualities of a good friend to Hassan. He offers comfort when a soldier boasts of having had sex with Hassan's mother: 'I reached across my seat, slung my arm around him, pulled him close… "He took you for someone else," I whispered' *(Chapter 2)*. It is Amir who carves their names into the pomegranate tree and also Amir who declares his love openly, "You're a prince and I love you" *(Chapter 4)*. However, Amir is equally capable of cruelty. He exploits and mocks Hassan's lack of education and can be rude to him, simply to satisfy the sense of jealousy he feels when Hassan receives affection from Baba. This mean-spiritedness brings Amir pleasure and reproach from readers. Amir's loyalty test of Hassan in Chapter 6 is another of these rather cruel behaviours. It is also self-indulgent and unnecessary, given that Hassan's loyalty has been proven countless times before. More than this, when the tables are turned, Amir's duplicitous nature is revealed: 'that's the thing about people who mean everything they say. They think everyone else does too' *(Chapter 6)*.

Key quotations

"Amir and Hassan, the sultans of Kabul" *(Chapter 4)*

…there was something fascinating—albeit in a sick way—about teasing Hassan. *(Chapter 6)*

Betrayal and guilt

Amir's testing of Hassan's loyalty is deeply ironic given what happens on that 'frigid overcast day' in the alleyway *(Chapter 1)*. His failure to act becomes the defining moment in his life, and Hassan becomes the focus around which Amir's existence subsequently revolves and through which all his other relationships are filtered and understood. Although not religious, Amir interprets his actions on that day through religious readings. He claims that his abandonment of Hassan is not merely cowardice but rather a conscious and deliberate act on his part in order to win his father's acceptance. If Hassan's loyalty knows no bounds, neither does Amir's ruthlessness at this point. His first reaction is to scan the last, fallen kite for damage and he is thankful there is none, which juxtaposes the soiled and ripped clothes of Hassan. In his selfishness, he is relieved that Hassan does not cry while in front of him, and finally he has his father's approval so his actions can be erased and forgotten: 'I forgot what I'd done. And that was good' *(Chapter 7)*.

It proves, however, to be the hollowest of victories. Such is the intensity of the shame, guilt and disgust that engulf Amir that he quickly realises that this is something he will carry with him forever. In the subsequent trip to Jalalabad with Baba, Amir is tortured by the vision of 'Hassan's brown corduroy pants discarded on a pile of old bricks in the alley' as he throws up at the roadside *(Chapter 8)*. Six years later as a refugee, Amir's mind flashes back to the sight of 'Assef's buttock muscles clenching and unclenching, his hips thrusting back and forth' *(Chapter 10)*. Even in the USA, Amir's demons persistently follow and the scars remain raw, although he claims it is a place where he can 'bury my memories' *(Chapter 11)*. On the night of his graduation, Baba's disappointment that Hassan is not present makes Amir feel like 'A pair of steel hands closed around' his windpipe *(Chapter 11)*. Soraya's tale of helping the family's maid read letters prompts Amir to consider how 'I had used my literacy to ridicule Hassan' *(Chapter 12)*. Her confession about her past brings the memory of how he had 'betrayed Hassan, lied, driven him out' *(Chapter 12)*.

Amir's greatest successes, such as news that his first book will be published, make him think about Hassan: *'Some day,* Inshallah, *you will be a great writer,* he had said once' *(Chapter 13)*. So do his greatest disappointments, such as Soraya's infertility: 'perhaps something, someone, somewhere, had decided to deny me fatherhood for the things I had done' *(Chapter 13)*. Burned as he is into Amir's conscience, Hassan is everywhere no matter where Amir may be.

Amir's feelings about Hassan are very complex and he carries the guilt of letting Hassan down wherever he goes

> **Key quotation**
>
> Nothing was free in this world. Maybe Hassan was the price I had to pay, the lamb I had to slay, to win Baba. *(Chapter 7)*

> **Activity 2**
>
> Look again at Chapter 7. Read from **'Then the moment came'** to **'...seeing Baba on that roof, proud of me at last'**. Write two paragraphs analysing how Hosseini conveys the intensity of this moment for Amir.

Redemption

However, if Hassan is the origin of Amir's spiral into ignominy and self-loathing, so is he the source of his redemption. In accepting and fulfilling Rahim Khan's opportunity to *'be good again' (Chapter 1)*, Amir succeeds in rescuing Sohrab, paying his debt to Hassan and redeeming himself. His incredible bravery and courage in re-entering Afghanistan, tracking down Sohrab and fighting Assef emulates that of his father. Through his actions he also reconciles himself with Baba and redeems his father's sins. As part of this process, in returning with Sohrab to the USA, Amir also completes his 'family' and assumes the role of the father he never thought he would be.

Amir – teller of stories

Reading and writing are fundamental aspects of Amir's life. In his childhood, it brings him closer to his dead mother, a teacher of literature, and offers a place of refuge from his distant, critical father. Hassan and Rahim Khan both play important roles in encouraging Amir as a writer. Reading is a favourite pastime of the two young boys and it is Hassan's reaction to Amir improvising a story of his own, **"That was the best story you've read me in a long time"** *(Chapter 4)* that actually inspires him to write his first short story. Despite the complete lack of interest from Baba, Rahim Khan's *'Bravo'*, according to Amir, also **'did more to encourage me to pursue writing than any compliment any editor has ever paid me'** *(Chapter 4)*. His gift of a **'brown leather-bound notebook'** *(Chapter 8)* becomes one of Amir's prized possessions.

Amir succeeds as a professional writer in America. His first novel results in a five-city book tour and, with the advance for his second, he and Soraya put down a deposit on a bigger house. His latest book has received positive reviews but Wahid's interest in it embarrasses Amir, who is not writing about Afghanistan as Wahid would wish by telling **"the rest of the world what the Taliban are doing to our country"** *(Chapter 19)*. However, he does later clearly take up and act upon Wahid's suggestion that he write about his native country. In doing so, Amir is telling his story, which becomes an act of **catharsis** for himself and for Afghanistan.

catharsis the act of releasing intense or repressed emotions

Activity 3

a) There are frequent references to Amir being car sick. Identify these and explain what it suggests about him.

b) During the journey from Peshawar to Islamabad with Farid and Shorab, Amir is not car sick. Why is this significant?

Baba

Force of nature

Baba is Amir's and also Hassan's biological father. His name in Arabic means 'father'. He is portrayed as a physically powerful, popular man who is successful in business and highly respected by his community. Living in the politically stable Afghanistan of Zahir Shah, Baba is liberal in his thinking, open in his opposition to religious intolerance, and enjoys more western practices such as drinking alcohol and throwing lavish parties. His physical prowess is emphasised through Amir's description of him as 'a towering Pashtun specimen' with 'hands that looked capable of uprooting a willow tree' *(Chapter 3)* and also through the story of him wrestling 'a black bear in Baluchistan with his bare hands' *(Chapter 3)*. Scars on his back prove the veracity of the story for Amir and such activities are not uncommon in countries like Afghanistan. There can be no doubt about his charismatic and winning personality. Amir's assertion that 'when all six-foot-five of him thundered into the room, attention shifted to him like sunflowers turning to the sun' *(Chapter 3)* is supported by Rahim Khan's description that this is a man who could "drop the devil to his knees begging for mercy" with no more than 'a black glare' *(Chapter 3)*.

Baba is a man who likes a challenge and enjoys defying the odds. This is seen in him becoming 'one of the richest merchants in Kabul' *(Chapter 3)*; marrying Amir's mother who at the time was 'universally regarded as one of Kabul's most respected, beautiful, and virtuous ladies' and 'a descendant of the royal family' *(Chapter 3)*; and building an orphanage, which causes those who doubted him to shake 'their heads in awe at his triumphant ways' on its completion *(Chapter 3)*. Baba is a man, according to Amir, who 'molded the world around him to his liking' *(Chapter 3)*. Everything, that is, except Amir.

Distant father

Baba is a distant father to Amir. He cannot hide his disappointment in him and is caught voicing these thoughts aloud to Rahim Khan. This is a significant moment because it means that Amir's perceptions of him are accurate. Amir lacks not only the physical strength of his father but also his personality and courageousness. This is compounded further by Amir having no interest in or, worse, being repulsed by Baba's hobbies such as buzkashi. In return, Baba shows disdain for Amir's interest in books and writing. His rejection of Amir's first story by not even reading it is at best insensitive and at worst cruel.

Activity 4

a) Baba is the Arabic word for 'father'. Explain why Hosseini uses this as the name of Amir's father.

b) Find references to when Baba behaves coldly towards Amir and warmly towards Hassan.

Honour and guilt

Baba is the man who risks his life to prevent the rape of a woman by an unscrupulous Russian soldier as her husband sits fearfully by doing nothing. For him, **"respect, honor"** are everything *(Chapter 10)*. This episode and his words to Amir during it, as he slaps the hands of his terrified son away – **"Haven't I taught you anything?"** *(Chapter 10)* – reveal his darkest concern, which is that Amir is a coward who will not stand up for what is right. This echoes his previous words to Rahim Khan, **"A boy who won't stand up for himself becomes a man who can't stand up to anything"** *(Chapter 3)*. If these words are prophetic in light of Chapter 7, those spoken during the incident with the Russian soldier only reinforce what has already taken place and the gulf between the father and son.

Baba's treatment of Amir is better understood by two things: the loss of his wife and his fathering of Hassan. Amir, particularly given his enjoyment of reading and writing, is a constant reminder of the wife he loved and lost so early in their relationship. It does not excuse his treatment of Amir but helps to contextualise it. More important though is the revelation that Baba's illicit affair with Sanaubar resulted in Hassan. Amir cannot be privy to the internal conflict that exists within his father as a result of this, which is why Rahim Khan's letter to Amir in Chapter 23 is so important, revealing Baba's turmoil as **'a man torn between two halves'** *(Chapter 23)* – Amir and Hassan. Amir is one half of this reflection of Baba, showing **'the socially legitimate half, the half that represented the riches he had inherited and the sin-with-impunity privileges that came with them'** *(Chapter 23)*. This makes clear that Baba's distance from Amir and his harsh treatment of him is a form of self-punishment for his own failings as a man, a husband and a father.

In addition, this also contextualises his generosity to those begging on the street and his charity work such as the construction of the orphanage – all acts designed to redeem himself for his shameful actions many years before. Similarly, it also casts his advice to Amir in a new light. At the time of its telling, his sermon about stealing is a powerful one: **'there is only one sin, only one. And that is theft. Every other sin is a variation of theft'** *(Chapter 3)*. In light of his actions, it could be seen as grotesque hypocrisy. However, it is better explained in the context of Rahim Khan's letter, as genuine advice from a father who had learned from his own mistakes to a son who he hopes will avoid doing the same. Tellingly, Baba has no romantic relationships after his dalliance with Sanaubar.

Key quotations

"I'll take a thousand of his bullets before I let this indecency take place" *(Chapter 10)*

...when your father was hard on you, he was also being hard on himself *(Chapter 23)*

Life in the United States

Baba's circumstances in America greatly contrast with those he enjoyed in Afghanistan. Apart from significant language and cultural barriers, his social circle, status and business successes, built up over many years, vanish overnight. He is unsuited to the conditions. It is in America that he develops cancer and dies. However, there are glimpses of the man he used to be. His sense of pride remains, evident in his refusal to live off welfare. His determination and business acumen are apparent in gaining a manager's position at the petrol station and making extra revenue through selling at the flea market.

Baba in the 2007 film

The old charisma returns in the bar on the night of Amir's high school graduation where 'just like that, Baba had started a party' *(Chapter 11)*. More importantly, it is in America that Baba once more finds pride in his son and also learns to appreciate his writing. Amir and Baba are never closer than they are on that foreign soil.

Key quotation

But the Bay Area's smog stung his eyes, the traffic noise gave him headaches, and the pollen made him cough. The fruit was never sweet enough, the water never clean enough, and where were all the trees and open fields? *(Chapter 11)*

Function in the novel

Baba's character contributes significantly to a number of key themes such as the relationship between fathers and their sons; sin and redemption; what it means to be a man; religion and ethnicity; and immigration. He also represents many of the positive attributes of the Afghan people: generosity of spirit, physical strength, a strong sense of morality, business acumen, independence and fearlessness. In his failings and struggles to put them right, he represents humanity.

> ### Activity 5
>
> **a)** How important to Amir's development is it that Baba dies when he does?
>
> **b)** By the end of the novel, how are Baba and Amir alike?

Hassan

Ethnicity

Hassan is a Hazara servant boy, son of Ali, biological son of Baba and childhood friend of Amir. His Mongol ancestry is reflected in his appearance. Another important physical aspect is his cleft lip, which Baba has reconstructed.

Hassan is present from Chapter 1 to Chapter 8, when he and Ali depart the house. Rahim Khan fills in details about Hassan's life in the intervening years in Chapter 16 and Hassan's voice is finally heard once more in his letter to Amir in Chapter 17. Despite this, Hassan is a constant presence throughout the novel and of central importance to it.

Being Hazara, Hassan is a member of a persecuted community that faces continual discrimination and sectarian violence. Even Amir can resort to such insults when irritated. Hassan's criticism of his first story provokes the remark, *'What does he know, that illiterate Hazara?'* (Chapter 4). But the attitude is best illustrated in the character of Assef, who says of Hassan, **"We are the true Afghans, the pure Afghans […] His people pollute our homeland, our *watan*. They dirty our blood"** *(Chapter 5)*. This mindset allows the later destruction of their religious temples and their mass slaughter by the Taliban.

> **Key quotation**
>
> ...his almost perfectly round face, a face like a Chinese doll chiseled from hardwood... *(Chapter 2)*

Loyal servant

Hassan, like his father, accepts his social status and life of servitude. This is evident in his refusal to sleep in the house once he returns to Kabul with Rahim Khan. Ingrained over time and perhaps deepened by a sense of obligation to Amir's grandfather for taking in the orphaned Ali, Hassan is absolutely dedicated as a servant. His loyalty in all things to Amir is an extension of that. The boys enjoy a very close friendship despite the social and religious barriers between them. Most striking in everything they do is Hassan's selflessness: he takes the blame for their mischievous pranks; he fights for Amir when Amir will not fight for himself. Hassan is raped to ensure that Amir gets the final fallen kite and Baba's affection. Hassan also accepts the allegations of theft, which are not true, to save Amir from embarrassment. He is the epitome of loyalty. His words *'For you, a thousand times over'* (Chapter 1) could sound bombastic and sensationalist, but are anything but that. One powerful image is that of Hassan later 'serving drinks to Assef and Wali from a silver platter' (Chapter 8), dutifully and without complaint or protest. Even more powerful is the image of Hassan's eyes as those of the sacrificial lamb in Amir's guilt-induced visions.

Activity 6

What does the slingshot represent for Hassan?

Activity 7

Look again at Chapter 7. Read from 'He had the blue kite in his hands' to 'He turned from me and limped away'. How does Hosseini create sympathy for Hassan in this extract?

Figure of goodness and redeemer of others

Hassan accepts his position and endures pain for Amir because he is secure psychologically. His relationship with his father is a warm and loving one. He accepts his role in society, is not driven by material gain and his ambitions are humble. Hassan has great faith too and throughout the story he is presented as content. He is said to have been born smiling and his actions show him to be a model of goodness. Hassan has the ability to forgive Amir the great injustices he has done him both as a child – "I don't know what I've done, Amir agha. I wish you'd tell me" (Chapter 8) – and as an adult – 'you will find an old faithful friend waiting for you' (Chapter 17). This is reinforced in his forgiveness of his mother, despite her outright rejection of him when he was born. Sanaubar is disgusted at the sight of the newborn infant whom she labels an 'idiot' and she 'refused to even hold' him (Chapter 2). However, after some reflection at the pomegranate tree, Hassan welcomes and forgives her without question, allowing her to redeem herself for her past wrongs. Hassan's goodness becomes a channel through which those who have committed wrongdoing can atone for it.

Hassan's history, as revealed by Rahim Khan and his letter to Amir, confirms that Amir's portrayal is reliable. As an adult, Hassan is the same good-natured, respectful, humble and religious soul he was as a child. He is a success, albeit within the context of his social class. Although living in poverty in Hazarajat when found by Rahim Khan, Hassan is happily married.

A scene of domestic bliss and security is portrayed shortly after his return to Kabul. Rahim Khan describes the 'haven' (Chapter 17), created within the confines of the home, which contrasts with the war raging outside. Hassan slips easily into the role of his father years before. He also becomes 'a very proud and very lucky father' (Chapter 17) to his son after suffering the loss of his first child, a stillborn daughter. In this, he is very much like his own father. Hassan and Sohrab spend their time doing the same things Hassan and Amir did – reading the *Shahnamah* under the pomegranate tree and kite flying.

His death at the hands of the Taliban is revealed dramatically but is a necessary event if Amir is to be redeemed. Once again, even in death, Hassan sacrifices himself for Amir. The novel requires that Sohrab becomes orphaned so he can be rescued by Amir and taken back to the USA, where he becomes the son that Amir and Soraya cannot have. Hassan's death facilitates all of this.

Function in the novel

Hassan enables readers to understand the life and predicament of the minority Hazara. He is the embodiment of goodness and facilitates the redemption of others. Symbolically, Hassan can also be seen to represent Afghanistan; he exemplifies the type of forgiveness that will be required by its people if they are to ever live together in peace.

Ali

Ali's is Hassan's non-biological father and Baba's childhood friend. He is the character who might be considered to suffer most in the novel. Being Hazara, he is already a member of a minority. His parents were run over by two brothers, drunk and high on drugs, leaving him orphaned. Polio has resulted in facial disfigurement, a withered arm and an atrophied leg, which means 'It seemed a minor miracle he didn't tip over with each step' *(Chapter 2)*. Physical affliction is often regarded in religious terms as a character-building trial from God. Bearing such affliction with fortitude therefore marks Ali out as fundamentally good. However, it makes him the victim of relentless bullying and name-calling by the local children and by Assef in particular. His first wife leaves him for another man after three years and his second wife, Sanaubar, is openly scathing of his appearance and abandons him straight after Hassan's birth. Baba fathers Hassan, betraying their friendship and, after the attack on Hassan, Ali is forced out of the house and into an uncertain future, all the while knowing that Hassan is innocent of the theft he is charged with. Incredibly, Ali bears all of this without complaint and with great fortitude. Eventually, he is killed by stepping on a landmine.

Like Hassan, Ali is a deeply religious man who simply accepts his personal circumstances and social status, forgiving those who act against him. He is a devoted and loving father. This is evident in the fact that he acquiesces to Hassan's request not to contradict Amir's lies in the showdown with Baba. He also remains loyal to Baba despite 'knowing he had been dishonoured by his master in the single worst way an Afghan man can be dishonoured' *(Chapter 18)*.

It is clear to see where Hassan's qualities and personal attributes come from and Ali's relationship with Baba is a reflection of that between Amir and Hassan. Ali's words, 'there was a brotherhood between people who have fed from the same breast, a kinship that not even time could break' *(Chapter 2)* in reference to Hassan and Amir, are deeply prophetic. The boys are tied to each other over subsequent years and across geographical distances and even in death; none of which can separate them.

> **Key quotation**
>
> ...Ali was immune to the insults of his assailants; he had found his joy, his antidote, the moment Sanaubar had given birth to Hassan. *(Chapter 2)*

Function in the novel

Ali represents the Hazara people, the oppression they have had to endure and the idea of purity and goodness. His character contributes to a number of themes, especially that of fathers and sons.

> ### Activity 8
>
> What is the significance of the names Ali and *Babalu*?

> ### Activity 9
>
> Which other characters are physically marked or afflicted to show their goodness?

Rahim Khan

Rahim Khan is Baba's closest friend and business partner. Their relationship is such that Rahim Khan is **'the only person'** *(Chapter 3)* who can criticise Baba. On one occasion he tells him, **"You know, sometimes you are the most self-centred man I know"** *(Chapter 3)*. Rahim Khan is a loyal friend who does not judge. He keeps Baba's secret and maintains their friendship when others might have walked away or gossiped about it. He appreciates that human beings make bad choices in life.

There is also a certain mystery to Rahim Khan. His background is never discussed and he is a solitary figure who never married. He is, though, a positive presence in Amir's life and acts as a surrogate father, providing the attention, advice and encouragement his own father fails to give. Interestingly, in a photograph as an infant, Amir is in Baba's arms but says, **'it's Rahim Khan's pinky my fingers are curled around'** *(Chapter 2)*. When Baba shows little interest in Amir's first story, it is Rahim Khan who steps in. Amir's choice of words is telling: **'As always, it was Rahim Khan who rescued me. He held out his hand and favored me with a smile that had nothing feigned about it'** *(Chapter 4)*. His subsequent note is full of praise for Amir's efforts and, momentarily, Amir **'wished Rahim Khan had been my father'** *(Chapter 4)*. The closing words in his note are also prescient. He tells the young Amir, **'I shall hear any story**

Rahim Khan always encouraged the young Amir

you have to tell' *(Chapter 4)*. Ultimately, however, Amir is unable to tell even Rahim Khan his most important story.

Khan is a wise man who sees the good in people despite their failings. This is the case with both Baba and Amir. He becomes the trigger for Amir's redemption when he calls and requests he visit him in Pakistan. Khan wants an end to the cycle of betrayal, lies and all its consequences of which he was a part.

Function in the novel

Rahim Khan plays an important role by narrating the details of Hassan's life in the years that Amir has been away. He also reveals the horrors of life in Kabul as the civil war raged and the Taliban came to power. In terms of the Bildungsroman genre, Rahim Khan fulfils the function of the guide and mentor to the young protagonist who helps him see with greater clarity what responsibilities he must accept and act upon.

> **Key quotation**
>
> *There is a way to be good again... (Chapter 18)*

Activity 10

a) Why does Rahim Khan tell Amir about his love for a Hazara woman in Chapter 8?

b) To what extent is Rahim Khan seeking atonement for himself through Amir?

c) Does Rahim Khan live up to the meaning of his name, which is compassionate and merciful?

Sohrab

Sohrab first appears in Chapter 16. He is Hassan's son and there is a very strong physical resemblance between Sohrab and his Amir describes their resemblance as 'breathtaking' *(Chapter 22)*. There are other similarities, such as Sohrab's religious beliefs and his accuracy with a slingshot.

In rescuing Sohrab from sexual slavery at the hands of the evil Assef, Amir finds redemption. Sohrab is subsequently a passive character as Amir recovers from his injuries and tries to find a way to adopt him and take him back to America. That is until Sohrab's attempted suicide, which is borne out of desperation to escape the traumatic experiences in his life. He is clearly less able to accept his situation than Hassan and Ali before him. His silence and withdrawn nature are tempered only by the faint hint of a smile at the novel's conclusion.

Function in the novel

Sohrab is the means by which Amir achieves redemption. He further represents an Afghanistan that can no longer take the violence and brutality being inflicted upon it.

Alternatively, he could be seen to represent the Hazara people and the fact that they can endure no more oppression. More positively, his faint smile at the end offers some semblance of hope for both.

Assef

Assef is the childhood bully and sadist who becomes an adult mass murderer. Amir describes him as a sociopath (a person with a personality disorder resulting in extreme antisocial attitudes and behaviour). He has no redeeming features. As a child, 'His well-earned reputation for savagery preceded him on the streets' *(Chapter 5)*. Amir identifies his sociopathic tendencies when recounting how he beats a child unconscious. These tendencies are also evident in Assef's praise of Hitler, which, with his German ancestry and physical appearance, closely associate him with Nazism and the Aryan race. Assef is Ali's chief tormentor and, in a twisted attempt to denigrate Hassan, he rapes him because he is 'just a Hazara' *(Chapter 7)*. His sexual abuse of Sohrab continues this line of generational degradation, reflecting the years of oppression endured by the Hazara.

> **Key quotation**
>
> ...Assef's blue eyes glinted with a light not entirely sane and how he grinned, how he *grinned*, as he pummeled that poor kid unconscious. *(Chapter 5)*

Assef's hatred of 'all the dirty, *kasseef* Hazaras' *(Chapter 5)* and his sociopathic nature find a perfect home in the Taliban, which provides political and religious cover for his actions. Assef talks with a perverted sense of spiritual fulfilment about his involvement in the Hazara massacre at Mazar-i-Sharif. However, the sunglasses he wears are a typically western fashion accessory and, combined with his predilection for the sexual abuse of children, he is clearly presented as a hypocrite.

Function in the novel

Assef acts as Amir's antagonist, the opposing force he must overcome to secure his own redemption and development. Symbolically, he also represents the dangers of radical religious fundamentalism and the abuse of Afghanistan.

Activity 11

How does Hosseini further reflect Assef's hypocrisy in Chapter 22?

Activity 12

In what ways are Amir and Assef similar?

Soraya

Soraya is Amir's wife, an immigrant and the daughter of a decorated Afghan general. She and Amir meet at the flea market and he is immediately taken by her beauty: 'I'd think of the shadow her hair cast on the ground when it slid off her back and hung down like a velvet curtain' *(Chapter 12)*.

Their courtship follows the strict traditions of Afghan culture, which requires Baba to seek formal permission from her father for Amir to marry his daughter before they have even dated. This formality is heightened further by Soraya's past, for she had previously run away and lived with a man when the family lived in Virginia. Such behaviour shamed the family to the extent that her father threatened to kill himself and her lover if she did not return. This incident reveals the strict codes that govern life for Afghan women but also an independent streak in Soraya that brings her into conflict with her father and culture. She rails against the double standards that mean that Afghan males can do as they please.

This image of Soraya and Sohrab at the end of the film promises hope for the future

Soraya is keen to explain her past to Amir before he fully commits to her. This suggests an honesty and bravery that juxtaposes Amir's lack of both. Soraya is compassionate and nurses Baba through his illness, too. Kind and intelligent, she becomes a teacher like Amir's mother. It is clear that Soraya and Amir have a loving relationship and a successful life. Her infertility, though, means they cannot have children, which causes them both great heartache. There is a certain irony here in that the most developed of all the female characters, who desperately wishes to be a mother, is not allowed to be. Ultimately, though, the arrival of Sohrab offers her this chance.

Function in the novel

Soraya is an important aspect of Amir's maturation process and is portrayed positively. She also allows exploration of Afghan attitudes towards women. Her name is the same as the wife of Amanullah Khan, who led Afghanistan after the third Anglo-Afghan war. She championed women's issues at a time when Afghanistan was stable and peaceful. In light of this, Soraya is also associated with hope and women's rights.

> **Key quotation**
>
> "Their sons go out to nightclubs looking for meat and get their girlfriends pregnant, they have kids out of wedlock and no one says a goddamn thing. Oh, they're just men having fun! I make one mistake and suddenly everyone is talking *nang* and *namoos*, and I have to have my face rubbed in it for the rest of my life." *(Chapter 13)*

Activity 13

a) What is the significance of the sickle-like birthmark above Soraya's jaw?

b) In what ways do Soraya and Hassan share similar experiences and characteristics?

Sanaubar

Sanaubar is Hassan's mother; Hassan was the result of her affair with Baba. Her sexual allure is strongly emphasised: her face **'tempted countless men into sin'** and her **'suggestive stride and oscillating hips sent men to reveries of infidelity'** *(Chapter 2)*. She is portrayed as acting on this for she is a **'notoriously unscrupulous woman who lived up to her dishonourable reputation'** *(Chapter 2)*. This seems to be evidenced by her illicit act with Baba while married to Ali and also by the soldier's upsetting comments to Hassan. Her negative portrayal is reinforced by her disgust and contempt for Ali, for she is repulsed by his appearance and **'joined the neighborhood kids in taunting'** her husband *(Chapter 2)*. Her instant rejection of Hassan and abandonment of husband and son further underlines this negative portrayal.

Sanaubar flees with a troupe of travelling singers and dancers, but many years later she returns during Rahim Khan's narration. She is described in stark contrast to her youth as **'a toothless woman with stringy graying hair and sores on her arms. She looked like she had not eaten for days. But the worst of it by far was her face. Someone had taken a knife to it'** *(Chapter 16)*. It can be assumed that her notorious sexual allure has been the cause of this facial mutilation. Sanaubar has come seeking forgiveness and redemption, which Hassan facilitates, but only after a night of agonising reflection. She is clearly sorry for rejecting her son all those years ago: **"Allah forgive me, I wouldn't even hold you"** *(Chapter 16)*.

Sanaubar is nursed back to health, reunites with Hassan and also delivers Sohrab in scenes that reflect domestic happiness in a simple and humble life. She finally dies in her sleep. Having reconciled with Hassan, she is described as looking **'calm, at peace, like she did not mind dying now'** *(Chapter 16)*.

Function in the novel

Sanaubar contributes to the themes of motherhood, the mistreatment of women and redemption.

> **Key quotations**
>
> ...in her youth, she was a vision. She had a dimpled smile and a walk that drove men crazy. No one who passed her on the street, be it a man or a woman, could look at her only once. *(Chapter 16)*
>
> ...I would look out the window into the yard and watch Hassan and his mother kneeling together, picking tomatoes or trimming a rosebush, talking. They were catching up on all the lost years, I suppose. *(Chapter 16)*
>
> I remember Sanaubar came out of the hut holding her grandson [...] She stood beaming under a dull gray sky, tears streaming down her cheeks, the needle-cold wind blowing her hair, and clutching that baby in her arms like she never wanted to let go. Not this time. *(Chapter 16)*

Activity 14

Write a paragraph explaining how Sanaubar contributes to the theme of motherhood, using quotations to support your opinions.

Sofia Akrami

Sofia is Amir's mother but dies giving birth to him. It is clear that Amir misses her greatly, his pain made worse by his father's distance and Amir's belief that he is responsible for her death. Although Amir states that he 'hadn't grown up around women' *(Chapter 13)*, this is not the case because his mother is a major influence on him through her books, which encourage a love of reading and writing in her son. Her history books about the Hazara also reveal a religious tolerance and liberal outlook.

Sofia is described in the most positive terms and, for Amir, she becomes a symbol of love and purity. This is reinforced by the old beggar he meets on returning to Kabul, who claims to have worked with her at the university and says of her, "Such grace, such dignity, such a tragedy" *(Chapter 20)*. The old man reveals her great happiness with life but also a prophetic anxiety in her belief that "They only let you be this happy if they're preparing to take something from you" *(Chapter 20)*.

Function in the novel

Sofia Akrami represents the idea that the dead can still influence the living powerfully.

> **Key quotation**
>
> ...a highly educated woman universally regarded as one of Kabul's most respected, beautiful, and virtuous ladies. And not only did she teach classic Farsi literature at the university, she was a descendant of the royal family... *(Chapter 3)*

General Sahib (Iqbal Taheri)

General Sahib is the husband of Khanum Taheri and father of Soraya. He was formerly a decorated general who worked for the Afghan Defence Ministry and now finds himself an immigrant in the USA. He is portrayed as officious and insincere. Amir comments how his lavish praise of his father 'sounded to me the way his suit looked: often used and unnaturally shiny' *(Chapter 11)*. He is uncomfortable out of his natural environment and eager to return to Afghanistan and his position of power and social standing.

Most of all, General Sahib is intent on ensuring that Afghan traditions are upheld to avoid any shame being brought on his family. This is particularly so following Soraya's elopement with a man. While this would not have caused much concern in the USA, it is enough to drive General Sahib into a violent, threatening rage. Such cultural tensions are expressed through the General's migraines and his taking antidepressants. Unlike Baba, the General is happy to live off welfare, feeling that the type of employment available is beneath him. There is also his underlying racism towards Sohrab, which Amir very publically reprimands in Chapter 25. The General eventually returns to Afghanistan and his ministry position by the book's conclusion.

Function in the novel

General Sahib reflects traditional Afghan customs and the male's position of privilege within Afghan society.

> **Key quotation**
>
> The general believed that, sooner or later, Afghanistan would be freed, the monarchy restored, and his services would once again be called upon. *(Chapter 13)*

Activity 15

How does Hosseini symbolically reflect that the General is waiting for a return to Afghanistan?

Khanum Taheri (Khala Jamila)

Jamila is the General's wife and Soraya's mother. She encourages Amir's romantic interest in her daughter and is delighted that they marry, afraid that Soraya's previous relationship may have shamed the family and marked her out as undeserving of a husband within the immigrant Afghan community. For this reason she is said to adore Amir. She has previously suffered a stroke and, as a result, when she smiled Amir 'noticed the right side of her mouth drooping a little' *(Chapter 12)*. She subsequently becomes something of a hypochondriac, which draws mocking comments from the General.

Jamila's marriage to the General is a traditional Afghan one: he is in full control and her wishes are subservient to his. It was a condition of their marriage that she stop singing, which she very much enjoyed, as 'he believed the performing of it [was] best left to those with lesser reputations' *(Chapter 13)*. There is also a petty meanness in the General's treatment of her, for example in his rejection of her food, which makes her cry. They also sleep in separate bedrooms. She is, though, a positive figure, who is warm and kind.

Function in the novel

Khanum Taheri represents the traditional Afghan wife who is subservient to her husband but who is able to remain positive despite hardship.

Farid

Farid is the Tajik driver paid to take Amir back to Kabul to rescue Sohrab. During Amir's absence, Farid joined the Mujahideen as a child and fought the Soviets, losing several toes and fingers, his father and two daughters in the ensuing violence. Initially, Farid is contemptuous of Amir's claim to feel like a tourist on his return to his own country. He also scoffs at Amir's previous life of privilege, depicting an uncannily accurate picture of what it was like. He lambasts Amir, suspecting that he is in the country simply to sell land and return to the USA.

However, news of Amir's intention to save an orphaned boy draws an apology from Farid who, despite the dangers, becomes committed to helping him (albeit for payment). Despite his casual sectarianism, he is a decent man, as seen in his outrage with Zaman, the orphanage director. More tellingly, his use of the phrase "For you a thousand times over" *(Chapter 23)* aligns him powerfully with Hassan and brings Amir to tears.

Function in the novel

In turning away from violence, Farid can be seen to represent the rejection of it for a more peaceful solution to Afghanistan's problems. He also represents the Tajik, a separate ethnic group from the Pashtun and Hazara.

Minor characters

Farzana

Farzana is Hassan's wife and mother of Sohrab. She clearly loves Hassan and they are happy together despite their poverty. Farzana is gunned down by the Taliban while trying to protect Hassan. She is a positive female character who appears only briefly.

> **Key quotation**
>
> ...a shy woman, so courteous she spoke in a voice barely higher than a whisper... *(Chapter 16)*

Wahid

Wahid is Farid's brother. Amir spends one night in his home. Wahid offers generous hospitality, leaving his own family without food. He very publically chastises Farid for his rudeness towards Amir. Wahid is a decent, honourable man who embarrasses Amir by calling him "A true Afghan" *(Chapter 19)*, due to his mission to save Sohrab.

Raymond Andrews

Andrews is the American Embassy official in Islamabad whom Amir talks to about adopting Sohrab and returning with him to the USA. Amir is unimpressed by his curt and businesslike replies, mistaking his pragmatism and understanding of the complexities involved for a lack of interest. Amir assumes that he has no children, which he claims makes him unfit to do his job. The secretary later informs Amir that Andrews lost his daughter to suicide.

Omar Faisal

Andrews introduces Amir to Faisal, an immigration lawyer and personable man who thinks that what Amir is doing is "pretty great" (Chapter 24). However, Faisal is aware of the many obstacles stacked against Amir and advises that Sohrab be placed in a safe orphanage for a period while adoption proceedings begin – advice that Amir initially takes, with all its dire consequences.

Zaman

Zaman is the director of the orphanage in Kabul where Amir finds Sohrab. Initially, he is reluctant to help. However, 'caught between suspicion and hope' (Chapter 20), he does help. His revelation that a senior ranking Taliban official takes selected children away to sexually abuse them at will and currently has Sohrab is shocking and disgusting. Farid's reaction is to want to kill him, but Zaman is a good man who is trying to do his best in a terrible situation. His character makes readers question moral standards in a time of war and think about what is right and what is wrong.

Kaka Sharif

Sharif is Soraya's uncle and is first mentioned at her wedding to Amir in Chapter 13. He has been in the USA for more than 20 years by that time. A poet, he reads a poem dedicated to his niece at the ceremony. He also works at the Immigration and Naturalisation Service. It is his idea that Amir bring Sohrab to the USA and then begin adoption proceedings.

Tips for assessment

Upgrade

A good knowledge of the minor characters is important, as every character serves a function. Any one could be brought into your response to demonstrate how they contribute to the portrayal of a main character or to make clear how they help to develop a theme.

Kamal

Kamal is one of the two boys who hold Hassan down while Assef rapes him. He is clearly not interested in participating, although invited to do so. Content to subdue Hassan, he 'kept looking away' to avoid Assef's gaze (Chapter 7). He reappears later in the basement in Jalalabad with his father who, like Baba and Amir, is fleeing the Soviet invasion. He is a shadow of his former self:

'His eyes gave me a hollow look and no recognition at all registered in them' *(Chapter 10)*. Kamal has lost his mother to the violence and been the victim of gang rape himself: *'four of them… tried to fight'* *(Chapter 10)*. It is clear that he has lost the will to live and he dies on the journey to Peshawar.

Kamal's father

Kamal's father shoots himself in the head when he finds out that his son is dead. This follows the death of his wife three months previously and the rape of his son. He is an example of what war can do to a family and an individual. Before it, his family was safe and he ran a cinema in Kabul.

Wali

Wali is the other boy who assists Assef during the sexual assault. In the first encounter with Amir and Hassan, he is described as one of Assef's **'obeying friends'** *(Chapter 5)*, suggesting that he is easily dominated and controlled. He does not speak during this incident but watches with **'something akin to fascination'** *(Chapter 5)* as Hassan challenges and faces down Assef. In the second, brutal encounter, Wali is a more active participant who **'sounded unsure, excited, scared, all at the same time'** *(Chapter 7)*. He declines Assef's invitation to abuse Hassan as his father has told him such behaviour is **'sinful'**, and he is **'relieved'**, it can be assumed, that he has not been ordered to do it *(Chapter 7)*. Wali is obviously keen to be with Assef as a way to avoid becoming one of his victims.

Assef's parents

Assef's mother is German, which contextualises his knowledge of German politics and interest in Hitler. She is described as **'a small, nervous woman'** and his father is a **'short, lanky sort'** with an unconvincing laugh *(Chapter 8)*. Their demeanour at his party makes Amir wonder **'if maybe, on some level, their son frightened them'** *(Chapter 8)*, suggesting they are aware of their son's personality but unable to do anything about it.

Writing about characterisation

A good response will demonstrate clearly that characters are created deliberately to serve a specific function in the novel. It will show how characters are manipulated for Hosseini's own purpose through what they say and do, their appearance and the things they are associated with, as well as the language and imagery used to portray them.

Consider how characters present themselves, as well as how they are seen by other characters: this will reveal their complexities. Thinking about how a character develops during the story can also connect to the development of the plot or contribute to a key theme.

Hosseini's novel is a celebration of Afghanistan and simultaneously an education for the western reader about his place of birth. It honours the country's people, traditions and heritage. The spoken word is a vital part of any country's culture and Hosseini enables readers to connect more closely with Afghanistan by including words and phrases from the Pashto, Dari, Urdu, and Arabic. Their inclusion reflects the incredible ethnic diversity of the country – many Afghan people can switch freely from one language to another.

Reclaiming language

Hosseini is also reclaiming the languages used in Afghanistan, of which many in the West know little. The greeting *salaam alaykum* (peace be unto you) might be known and regarded positively, but, for some people in the West, phrases such as *Allah-u-Akbar* may have more negative connotations and be connected with Islamic terrorists, who are reported to use this call during their attacks. It is telling that the very first native phrase in the novel is precisely that: **'Allah-u-akbar'** *(Chapter 2)*. It means 'God is greater' and is used by Muslims during prayer and on many other occasions, formal and informal. The phrase is used as part of the act of worship and in day-to-day life to express gratitude to God for blessings. It acts as a reminder that, no matter what one's concerns are in life, God is greater than everything. Almost immediately, Hosseini is dramatically reclaiming this language from those who are intent on using it for evil purposes. In this novel, it becomes a celebration of life and religious devotion rather than a cry of death. This is reinforced by the fact that it appears in a tapestry hanging in the home of the humble, gracious Ali.

In the novel, the phrase *Allah-u-akbar* is a celebration of life

Educating readers

The novel is full of references to all aspects of Afghan life. Some of these, such as *naan* (a type of bread) are very likely to be already known to readers and are an indication of how immigrants enrich and diversify life in the countries in which they settle. Others, however, are unfamiliar. In such instances Hosseini provides a translation to ensure that meaning is not lost. For example, *laaf* is explained as **'that Afghan tendency to exaggerate'** *(Chapter 3)*.

On other occasions, Hosseini lets readers work out the meaning of the word from the context. When talking about the children, Zaman the Kabul orphanage director tells Amir, **"But they're not all *yateem*. Many of them have lost their fathers in the war, and their mothers can't feed them because the Taliban don't allow them to work"** *(Chapter 20)*. Clearly, *yateem* means orphan. There is little doubt about this as Zaman is responding to a question explicitly about orphans previously asked by Farid.

Activity 1

Find other examples of where Hosseini does not translate the native word and makes readers work it out for themselves. Why do you think Hosseini wants readers to do this?

Later, however, Hosseini removes these supports for readers and lets them rely solely on the context of the conversation to work out the meaning. For example, in a phone call with Amir, who is on his mission to rescue Sohrab and with whom she has not spoken for some time, Soraya says that she is *"sick with tashweesh!" (Chapter 24)*. This means 'worry'. The act of reading now becomes a doorway into the language used by Hosseini and the characters of his novel. Readers are forced to engage actively in using it too, through a process that requires increasing levels of independence.

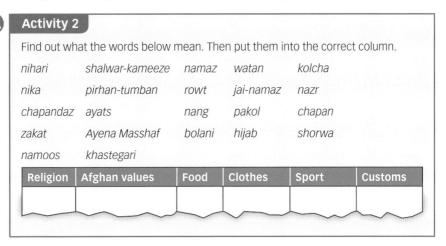

Activity 2

Find out what the words below mean. Then put them into the correct column.

nihari	shalwar-kameeze	namaz	watan	kolcha
nika	pirhan-tumban	rowt	jai-namaz	nazr
chapandaz	ayats	nang	pakol	chapan
zakat	Ayena Masshaf	bolani	hijab	shorwa
namoos	khastegari			

Religion	Afghan values	Food	Clothes	Sport	Customs

Challenging the West's domination of other states

Hosseini embraces his mother tongue throughout the novel. Although the novel is predominantly written in English, he elevates his native language to the same status as that of the English imposed on Afghanistan during the late 19th and early 20th centuries. He does this in several ways. For example, he introduces readers to the everyday, using words from languages such as Farsi and Pashto, which readers then have to engage with. He goes further by using Afghan words at important, emotionally charged points in the novel. On the day of the kite-fighting competition, as Amir hones in on victory and the tension rises, Hosseini has the crowd chanting *"Boboresh! Boboresh!" (Chapter 7)* as they encourage him to cut the string of the other kite. Later, in their encounter following Sohrab's attempted suicide, Amir is awash with guilt, having failed to keep his promise to Sohrab that he would not have to return to an orphanage – the trigger for Sohrab's attempt to end his own life. It is another pivotal moment in the novel, with Amir realising the extent of his responsibilities on his journey to redemption. Amir implores Sohrab for his 'bakhshesh' – forgiveness (Chapter 25). Sohrab's response offers little comfort as the boy simply states that he is "so *khasta*" – tired (Chapter 25).

In these ways, Hosseini challenges and reverses Britain and the West's domination of language and discourse. He includes the word *noor*, meaning 'light', in his dedication to his two children at the beginning of the novel, making his intentions clear from the very outset.

Creating distinct narrative voices

Just as people have their own **idiolect**, each individual character must also have their own distinctive voice. This is created through the words and phrases they use and how they express themselves. A writer must think carefully about crafting these different voices so they are believable and contribute purposefully to the novel. This is particularly so if the character has a role to play in narrating the story.

Amir

Amir narrates the vast majority of the novel. Given its retrospective nature, he is an adult at the time of writing. However, there is a childhood tone evident in the chapters that deal with those early years in Kabul. Amir recalls the opening of Baba's orphanage using simple and basic compound sentences. The vocabulary too is simplistic: '**When Baba ended his speech, people stood up and cheered. They clapped for a long time. Afterward, people shook his hand... I was so proud of Baba, of us**' (Chapter 3). Amir also employs childhood toys to make comparisons, so Hassan's face is like a Chinese doll, Baba's snoring is like a truck engine, and the sound of a rising kite is compared to the wings of a paper bird flapping, an indication of his childish mind at the time.

However, after the rape, this changes. The childlike narration disappears and comparisons are no longer made to childish things. Hassan's pomegranate-smeared face makes him look like '**he'd been shot by a firing squad**' (Chapter 8), evoking images of violence, war and death. As Hassan and Ali leave the house, Amir echoes Judas's betrayal of Jesus by comparing the rain to '**melting silver**' (Chapter 9). Cancer is described as being '**like Satan**' (Chapter 12). Amir's language during his time in the USA reflects his adulthood and also the impact of America on his language choices. Soraya's tale of double standards at the hands of the Afghan community for her ill-fated elopement draws a blunt "**Fuck 'em**" from Amir (Chapter 13).

> **direct address** when a writer talks directly to readers through the use of words like 'you' and 'your'
>
> **idiolect** the unique speech habits and patterns of an individual
>
> **lyricism** the use of heightened, poetic language to express deep emotions

Amir as professional writer

It is important to note that Amir is also a professional writer of fiction. He chooses metaphors to express himself, here using the imagery of water to express his fear that he will renege on his agreement to travel back and save Sohrab: **'I was afraid the appeal of my life in America would draw me back, that I would wade back into that great, big river and let myself forget, let the things I had learned these last few days sink to the bottom. I was afraid I'd let the waters carry me away from what I had to do'** *(Chapter 19)*. This captures his sense of fear and confusion while challenging the traditional idea of water as a cleansing and transformative agent.

Amir writes poetically too, capturing the atmosphere of an Afghan evening: **'I stepped outside. Stood in the silver tarnish of a half-moon and glanced up to a sky riddled with stars. Crickets chirped in the shuttered darkness and a wind wafted through the trees. The ground was cool under my bare feet'** *(Chapter 19)*. Later, he evokes the devastation visited upon Kabul by war: **'Jadeh Maywand had turned into a giant sand castle. The buildings that hadn't entirely collapsed barely stood, with caved in roofs and walls pierced with rocket shells. Entire blocks had been obliterated to rubble'** *(Chapter 20)*. There is a **lyricism**, too, in his description of Hassan, which makes clear his importance as a character in his life. His recalls **'sunlight flickering through the leaves on his almost perfectly round face, a face like a Chinese doll chiseled from hardwood'** and his eyes, which looked **'depending on the light, gold, green, even sapphire'** *(Chapter 2)*.

Activity 3

Find other examples of where Amir uses poetic language to talk about Hassan. What effect does this have on how you respond to Amir and also to Hassan?

Tense

Although writing about events that have already occurred, Amir's narration changes from the past to the present tense at specific moments. When the assault on Hassan happens, Amir switches to the present tense during his second memory and his dream sequence. This not only extends the scene but creates a somewhat disorientating effect on readers. This is deliberately designed to reflect the sense of swirling confusion and bewilderment that engulfs Amir. His reflection on the Eid-Al-Adha sacrifice of the lamb, which he associates with Hassan's eyes, is also related in the present tense. Here, it creates an immediacy that emphasises the horror of the attack taking place.

A similar effect is created in Chapter 10, when Amir is in the oil tanker being transferred to Peshawar: **'You open your mouth. Open it so wide your jaws creak. You order your lungs to draw air, NOW, you need air, need it NOW. But your airways ignore you. They collapse, tighten, squeeze, and suddenly you're breathing through a drinking straw'**. The present tense, once again, heightens the immediacy of Amir's terror and suffocation and brings readers closer to his predicament. The use of **direct address** and capitalisation add further impact.

In his fight with Assef, Amir employs the postmodern technique of reflecting the horror of his situation and the fragmentation of his mind by inserting a recollection of a doctor standing over him after the event, when in terms of chronology, the attack has not yet happened. Immediately after Assef removes his 'stainless-steel brass knuckles' from his pocket and his assault is about to begin *(Chapter 22)*, Amir cuts to the memory of the doctor treating him and how he 'has gel in his hair and a Clark Gable mustache above his thick lips' *(Chapter 22)*.

Although this gives a clear sense of Amir's fear, it is tempered by the knowledge that he must survive, whatever happens, as he is writing his book. Hosseini creates a sense of immediacy again by constantly using the **gerund** of the verb in grammatically incorrect sentences: 'That snapping sound yet again, now my nose. Biting down in pain, noticing how my teeth didn't align like they used to. Getting kicked. Sohrab screaming' *(Chapter 22)*. Although clearly writing about the past, readers are invited to feel each blow as though it is being struck for the first time, creating a much more powerful experience.

Rahim Khan

Rahim Khan's narration in Chapter 16 is that of an old man who is dying. In this regard, his frequent religious references are unsurprising, as his thoughts become more reflective and turn to God: 'Allah forgive me', 'I pray to Allah' and 'Allah was kind to us, though' *(Chapter 16)*. Despite his frailty, his anger is evident in his hatred of the Soviets, 'the *Shorawi*, may they rot in hell for what they did to our *watan*' *(Chapter 16)*.

Rahim Khan is obviously an educated man, evident in his sophisticated vocabulary – 'propaganda', 'glorified', 'illiterate' *(Chapter 16)* – and a lover of words and how they are used.

He employs the **rule of three** to good effect to emphasise his feelings of loneliness: 'No one to greet, no one to sit down with for *chai*, no one to share stories with, just *Roussi* soldiers patrolling the streets' *(Chapter 16)*. Later, he returns to this theme, employing a short dramatic sentence suggesting the depth of his isolation: 'An unbearable emptiness' *(Chapter 16)*.

He also captures the horrors of war through descriptive language and powerful images: 'Our ears became accustomed to the whistle of falling shells, to the rumble of gunfire, our eyes familiar with the sight of men digging bodies out of piles of rubble' *(Chapter 16)*.

> **gerund** the form of the verb ending in *-ing*
>
> **phallic symbolism** the use of objects to symbolise the male sexual organs
>
> **rule of three** a three-part structure designed to emphasise a point

Characters also have a speaking voice, the one they use to communicate with others in the novel. This reveals their thoughts and feelings, as well as the type of individual they are and the values they have. In his conversations with Amir, Rahim Khan reveals himself to be a kind, generous man who offers good advice and encouragement. When speaking with Baba, he is not afraid to offer criticism, sometimes bluntly.

Activity 4

a) Find quotations in Chapters 1–7 to contrast the way in which Baba and Rahim Khan speak to Amir.

b) Write two paragraphs contrasting the relationships both men have with Amir as a child.

Hassan

Hassan's narrative voice is heard in Chapter 17 in the letter he has written to Amir. His devoutly religious nature is strongly evident: 'In the name of Allah, the most beneficent, the most merciful […] I pray that this latest letter finds you in good health and in the light of Allah's good graces […] May Allah be with you always' *(Chapter 17)*. A rudimentary style reflects that Hassan has taught himself to read and write. The more sophisticated vocabulary of Rahim Kahn is missing. There is a tendency to use simple sentences – 'He is a good boy' *(Chapter 17)* – and basic compound sentences – 'I take Sohrab around Kabul sometimes and buy him candy' *(Chapter 17)*.

His narrative voice is also evident in the wording of sentences, some of which are rather awkwardly constructed – 'I have told much about you to Farzana jan and Sohrab' *(Chapter 17)* – while others have an unusual expression, in this case laced with religious influence: 'Perhaps a photograph of you will even grace our eyes' *(Chapter 17)*. Throughout, however, his humble nature is expressed through the simplicity of his writing: 'Rahim Khan sahib is quite ill. He coughs all day and I see blood on his sleeve when he wipes his mouth. He has lost much weight' *(Chapter 17)*.

Phallic symbolism

The rape of Hassan is a brutal act designed by Assef to inflict physical and psychological pain on another child. It is something that provoked much criticism of the novel, especially from Afghans, who took offence at the sexual violence. The writer uses **phallic symbolism** in the second memory, which alerts readers to what is to follow. Phrases such as "part the curtain of truth", 'silver embedded in deep, twin craters' and 'deflated cheeks' *(Chapter 7)* very subtly suggest the sexual act about to take place. Later, the dried blood on Assef's white shirt in Chapter 24 symbolises a loss of virginity – Amir's, for he is no longer the same innocent boy of that 'frigid overcast day' in 1975 *(Chapter 1)*.

Pathetic fallacy

Hosseini uses **pathetic fallacy** to reinforce theme. When Ali and Hassan leave the house with Baba for the bus station, the weather is biblical in its significance: 'Thunderheads rolled in, painted the sky iron gray. Within minutes, sheets of rain were sweeping in, the steady hiss of falling water swelling in my ears' *(Chapter 9)*. This suggests the traumatic severing of relationships and tumultuous action taking place. The word 'hiss' evokes the idea of snakes and recalls the serpent in the Garden of Eden tempting Eve and Adam into sin.

At the novel's conclusion, Amir awakes to raindrops which are 'pelting the window' on the day of the Afghan new year *(Chapter 25)*. Arriving at the park, people are 'taking cover' from it *(Chapter 25)*. However, 'By three o' clock, the rain had stopped' and 'A cool breeze blew through the park' *(Chapter 25)*. Later, Amir's description recalls his love of winter before Hassan's rape: 'The park shimmered with snow so fresh, so dazzling white, it burned my eyes. It sprinkled soundlessly from the branches of white-clad trees' *(Chapter 25)*. The cessation of the rain coupled with the positive, poetic description of the winter landscape sets the scene for the hint of engagement and reaction about to come from Sohrab, and Amir's resulting delight.

Activity 5

Find other examples of where Hosseini uses pathetic fallacy and explain their impact.

Symbolism

Slingshot

The slingshot draws on the biblical story of David and Goliath, in which the underdog defeats a much bigger enemy. It is most strongly associated with Hassan and Sohrab. Both are highly skilled in its use: Hassan 'was deadly with his slingshot' *(Chapter 2)* while Rahim Khan explains how 'by the time he was eight, Sohrab had become deadly with that thing' *(Chapter 16)*. The slingshot is more than just a childhood toy to distract young boys. Being Hazara and the victims of discrimination and abuse, it becomes a weapon necessary for protection.

Amir, who has his father's influence to protect him, does not own one. Hassan has taught his son to use the slingshot quite deliberately as a way to defend himself. Ironically, Hassan is not in possession of his slingshot on the day he is raped by Assef. Sohrab too, despite being inseparable from his, is unable to use it against the Kalashnikovs of Assef and the other Taliban members in the house where he is abused. However, both father and son use it to great effect to save Amir. On the first occasion, in Chapter 5, Hassan's cocked slingshot aimed at Assef's left eye is enough to deter

> **pathetic fallacy** a type of personification in which nature is given human characteristics to reflect the action and generate atmosphere

him from assaulting Amir. Later, in Chapter 22, 'The slingshot made a *thwiiiiit* sound when Sohrab released the cup' and then Assef 'put his hand where his left eye had been just a moment ago'. Once more, this basic but effective defensive device becomes the source of Amir's salvation.

The pomegranate tree

In Chapter 4, Amir carves the words "Amir and Hassan, the sultans of Kabul" on the pomegranate tree before eating the fruit and reading from the *Shahnamah*. At this stage, the tree and its fruit have positive associations of abundance, life and friendship.

After the rape, however, its symbolism changes dramatically. Amir next visits the tree at Hassan's request in Chapter 8 but soon realises he'd made a mistake and 'couldn't stand looking' at the names he had carved so eagerly. Clearly their friendship is ending. Their subsequent visit is instigated by Amir under false pretences and sees Amir pelt Hassan with pomegranates, hoping to secure the 'punishment I [he] craved' (Chapter 8). With no retaliation from Hassan, Amir is left rocking back and forth on his knees and in tears, their friendship now over.

Amir finally returns to the tree as an adult. This visit reveals the importance of Hassan to Amir. However, the tree is now dead and 'hadn't borne fruit in years' (Chapter 21), which symbolises the friendship that was lost. In locating the names and lovingly tracing the letters with his fingers, Amir, however, symbolically commits to Hassan and Sohrab.

Kites

Kites symbolise several things in the novel. They symbolise the friendship between Amir and Hassan; the 'twin' kites (Chapter 1) Amir sees at the start of the novel remind him of his time as a child flying kites with Hassan in Afghanistan and could be seen to represent the two boys themselves. Kites also represent the hope Amir feels during kite-flying season that he can become closer to Baba through his success as a kite flyer and achieve a 'happily ever after' (Chapter 7) ending to their unhappy and tense relationship.

There is also a darker side to kite flying: the glass-encrusted string and the violence of 'cutting' your opponents' kites suggests a more sinister element to this seemingly innocent pastime. When Hassan is raped by Assef for refusing to hand over the blue kite, it becomes a symbol of both Hassan's loyalty to Amir and of sacrifice – Hassan's self-sacrifice and Amir's willingness to sacrifice his friend in order to gain his father's love and esteem: 'the lamb I had to slay, to win Baba' (Chapter 7).

Amir hopes that his success at kite flying will earn Baba's love and respect

Mirrors

Initially, mirrors are used by Hassan and Amir to play childish pranks on their neighbours: **'by reflecting sunlight into their homes with a shard of mirror'** *(Chapter 2)*. In Ali's hands, a mirror is an instrument to punish and scare errant boys into better behaviour: **'He would take the mirror and tell us […] that the devil shone mirrors too, shone them to distract Muslims during prayer'** *(Chapter 2)*. Here its association with evil and disrupting religious worship is much more serious.

The connotations of mirrors become more positive as the novel develops and they become associated with the idea of truly knowing oneself and others. A mirror forms an important part of the **'Ayena Masshaf'** during Amir and Soraya's wedding, when the young lovers sit under a veil and stare at each other's reflection in a mirror *(Chapter 13)*. This custom was designed to allow some privacy at a traditional arranged wedding to those who had not met each other before. Even here, though, Amir cannot avoid thinking about Hassan and who he might have married: **'whose face he had seen in the mirror under the veil?'** *(Chapter 13)*. Later a nurse shows Amir his face in a mirror for the first time after his beating by Assef. It reflects the battered face of the man of courage, strength and morality that he has become.

Tips for assessment

Symbols are important and contribute significantly to the development of character and theme. They are not fixed in meaning, which can change as the novel develops. For example, the pomegranate tree is not merely a symbol of friendship; as Amir and Hassan's relationship changes, so too does the significance of the tree to reflect that. Symbols can also refer to more than one character or theme. As a symbol, the kite relates to both Amir and Hassan as well as the themes of friendship, sin and redemption.

Knuckledusters

These are an ever-present possession of Assef's, carried at all times in case the opportunity for gratuitous violence presents itself. They first appear in Chapter 5, when Amir recalls how Assef used them to beat one **'poor kid unconscious'**. On this occasion his **'blue eyes glinted with a light not entirely sane'** *(Chapter 5)*. This is later echoed in how **'His stainless-steel brass knuckles sparkled in the sun'** *(Chapter 5)* when produced for his intended assault on Amir, which requires Hassan's intervention. Here, sadist and instrument of torture become one through the imagery used to describe them. They appear again, during his wild assault on Amir in Chapter 23. They are also described as **'flashing in the afternoon light'** and Amir notes **'how cold they felt with the first few blows and how quickly they warmed with my blood'** *(Chapter 22)*. Assef does not simply want to inflict pain: he wants to inflict as much pain as possible and the knuckledusters allow that.

Motor vehicles

These either represent the individual's degree of social status or are associated with trauma and death in the novel. For example, Baba's black Ford Mustang in the early part of the novel symbolises his material wealth and status. In America, however, this is swapped for an **'old, ochre yellow Buick Century'** *(Chapter 11)*, which in turn is sold for a **'dilapidated '71 Volkswagen bus'** *(Chapter 11)*. Baba here exchanges the fashionable and expensive for what is practical and cheap. Amir himself compares the **'BMWs. Saabs. Porsches'** of the free world with the **'Russian Volgas, old Opels, or Iranian Paikans'** of Afghanistan *(Chapter 11)*. A further contrast can be drawn with Farid's functional but **'dilapidated Land Cruiser'**, which requires a screwdriver to wind down the window *(Chapter 19)*.

Motorised vehicles are also the cause of trauma and death. It is a Ford Roadster driven by two young Pashtun men drunk and high on drugs that kills Ali's parents. In **'the tarpaulin-covered cab of an old Russian truck'** smuggling Pashtun Afghans into Jalalabad *(Chapter 10)*, young Amir suffers the trauma of fearing that his father will be killed, and a young woman is saved from rape by Baba's intervention. The onward journey to Pakistan is completed in an empty oil tanker, the inside of which is **'pitch-black'** and whose **'air wasn't right, it was too thick, almost solid'** *(Chapter 10)*. The claustrophobic conditions provoke a panic attack in Amir and kill Kamal. Here, although associated with terrible events, traumatic personal experiences and loss, the truck also facilitates their escape from possible persecution and the freedom America can offer them.

Smiles

The importance of smiles, the human expression of happiness, revolves essentially around the characters of Hassan, Amir and Sohrab. In the novel a smile is a symbol of honesty, simplicity and redemption. It is a cruel twist of fate that the gentle and kind Ali **'had a congenital paralysis of his lower facial muscles, a condition that rendered him unable to smile and left him perpetually grim-faced'** *(Chapter 2)*. Hassan, in contrast, was born smiling. The corrected cleft lip prompts Amir to remark that the successful healing process **'was ironic. Because that was the winter that Hassan stopped smiling'** *(Chapter 5)*, referring to the impact of the rape and the subsequent events triggered by Amir's lies. However, Hassan does learn to smile again. In the photograph presented by Rahim Khan, Amir observes how **'the man in the *chapan* [Hassan] exuded a sense of self-assuredness, of ease [...] it was in the way he smiled. Looking at the photo, one might have concluded that this was a man who thought the world had been good to him'** *(Chapter 17)*. Sohrab is **'grinning'** too *(Chapter 17)*. In nature and temperament, Ali (despite his facial disfigurement), Hassan and Sohrab are very much alike. Hosseini presents three generations of the disadvantaged and oppressed Hazara as a continuation of all that is courageous, stoic and good. There is no doubt that Ali would smile often if he could, content with his life and what fate has dealt him.

Amir, on the other hand, despite his privilege, is estranged initially from his father, tortured by his actions and smiles very little. He comments how, after his assault by Assef and while trying to recover, he **'tried to smile and a bolt of pain ripped through my lips. I [Amir] wouldn't be doing that for a while'** *(Chapter 23)*. It is Sohrab, Hassan's son, who enables Amir to smile by the novel's conclusion when the sight of, and contact with, a kite produces a smile of sorts from the traumatised and mute child. It is **'Lopsided. Hardly there. But there'** *(Chapter 25)*. Finally, in a circular narrative and by having saved himself by saving the son of his half-brother, a child's faint smile offers hope for all concerned.

Cleft lip

The cleft lip unites Hassan and Amir, representing their brotherhood and the fact that Amir is, by the novel's conclusion, not only a reflection of his half-brother physically but also in terms of his personality. Hassan is born with the affliction but Baba's money corrects this as a birthday present, leaving **'only a faint scar'** *(Chapter 5)*. This places him firmly on the side of those, like Ali, who bear affliction as a sign of their morality and goodness. Having been assaulted by Assef, Amir's lip is cut **'Clean down the**

A cleft lip can be corrected successfully by surgery, if you have the money to pay for it

middle. Like a harelip' *(Chapter 23)*. This reflects the fact that Baba is their father and also now identifies Amir, like Hassan, as a man of courage and integrity.

Writing about language

When analysing language, better responses will confidently identify not only the specific parts of speech such as verbs, adjectives and adverbs, but also the relevant figures of speech such as simile, metaphor, personification, alliteration, assonance and onomatopoeia, among others. Once identified, their effect and purpose must be analysed in some detail: it is never enough to simply identify a list of features without exploring their purpose in the text.

Remember that Hosseini uses language for many different reasons, not just to tell the story. It reveals the details of his characters, creates meaning and contributes to the development of the themes at the heart of his novel. Consider how your chosen quotations reveal these ideas and then question why Hosseini uses the techniques he does.

Activity 6

a) Match each figure of speech to the correct definition and example from the novel in the table below.

Figure of speech	Definition	Example
1) simile	a) a number of words in a sentence starting with the same consonant and used deliberately	i) Then I glanced up and saw a pair of kites [...] They danced high above the trees... *(Chapter 1)*
2) metaphor	b) a word that, when spoken, sounds like the sound it gives its name to	ii) The scent of garbanzo beans in spicy sauce hung in the air, mixed with the smell of dung and sweat. *(Chapter 21)*
3) personification	c) a direct comparison in which one thing is said to be another	iii) At parties, when all six-foot-five of him [Baba] thundered into the room, attention shifted to him like sunflowers turning to the sun. *(Chapter 3)*
4) alliteration	d) when something inanimate is given the qualities of a living thing	iv) Suddenly I was hovering, looking down on myself from above. *(Chapter 7)*
5) onomatopoeia	e) the repetition of vowel sounds in a sentence, used deliberately	v) ...because Ali was immune to the insults of his assailants; he had found his joy, his antidote, the moment Sanaubar had given birth to Hassan. *(Chapter 2)*
6) assonance	f) a comparison of two unalike things that uses the words 'like' or 'as'	vi) The slingshot made a *thwiiiiit* sound when Sohrab released the cup. *(Chapter 22)*

b) Look at a student's analysis of the use of personification below. Using this example of how to analyse a figure of speech, write a paragraph explaining the use of each of the other five figures of speech listed in the table.

Amir uses personification to describe how he cannot escape his past, 'but it's wrong what they say about the past, I've learned, about how you can bury it. Because the past claws its way out.' The fact that the past is personified here is interesting in itself, suggesting that it is a living, breathing thing, an agent with its own mind and something that cannot be controlled. Moreover, use of the verb 'claws' suggests that it is animalistic and that its return is physically painful for Amir as it will rip and tear at his flesh in order to resurface. Used in conjunction with the verb 'bury', it creates associations with **psychoanalytic** interpretations, in that Amir has tried to escape his past by repressing and burying painful experiences and memories only to realise that he cannot. They will 'claw' themselves up from the depths of his memory.

psychoanalytic analysis relating to the study of how personality is organised and developed

Fathers and sons

Male relationships, and those between fathers and sons in particular, lie at the heart of the novel. Amir's relationship with his father is complex, compounded by the death of his mother and Baba secretly fathering Hassan. Grief and guilt drive Baba away from Amir, something the son cannot fully understand until near the novel's conclusion. According to Amir, it is his desire to get Baba's approval and love that prompts him to abandon Hassan in the alleyway. This proves only a temporary victory though, as Baba quickly reverts to disregarding his son.

In America, however, Baba and Amir eventually establish a more loving relationship. Away from Afghanistan and Hassan, it is easier for Baba to find pride in Amir. He not only shares this with his son, '"I am *moftakhir,* Amir," he said. Proud' (Chapter 11), but also celebrates it publicly, introducing Amir to General Taheri with the words "Amir is going to be a great writer" (Chapter 11). In America, he can do something not possible in Afghanistan – enjoy Amir's writing. They can even share tender moments: 'I reached across the table and put my hand on his' (Chapter 11).

> **Key quotation**
>
> By the end of the summer, the scraping of spoon and fork against the plate had replaced dinner table chatter and Baba had resumed retreating to his study after supper. And closing the door. (Chapter 8)

Ali and Hassan's relationship is a warm and loving one, which contrasts with the cold, fractured one of Baba and Amir. Although it is implied that Ali knows of Baba's betrayal, Hassan is clearly loved unconditionally by Ali and is presented as 'his joy' (Chapter 2). Ali manages this situation much better than Baba, who fails to acknowledge Hassan as his. His acts of kindness towards him serve to satisfy and maintain his guilty secret but leave Amir and Hassan ignorant of the truth. Ali and Hassan may be poor and powerless, but they juxtapose all that Baba and Amir have materially in what is essentially a loveless relationship while in Kabul.

Ali and Hassan's relationship is also echoed in that of Hassan's with Sohrab. This is depicted in very positive terms. Hassan, like Ali, is a devoted father, who has given his son all that his circumstances allow and more – the ability to read and write. He states that he is 'a very proud and very lucky father' (Chapter 17).

Amir's rescue of Sohrab later enables him to fulfil the role of fatherhood, which Soraya's infertility denies him. It is a role he is apparently well suited to do, hinted at by the hotel manager in Islamabad mistaking Sohrab for his son. Clearly, being a biological father is not a necessary requirement for being a good father.

> **Activity 1**
>
> What hints are there that Hassan is Baba's son before the revelation?

Sin and redemption

The theme of redemption is key to understanding the novel. Its importance is established on the very first page: 'unatoned sins' *(Chapter 1)*. Rahim Khan, Amir's surrogate father, initiates the road to redemption, not just for Amir but for Baba and himself with his telephone call. This suggests that despite his profound guilt, Amir could not have begun such a process himself.

Redemption requires sin and this takes various forms. There is Baba's betrayal of Ali in his lustful affair with Sanaubar. Cowardice and a desire for his father's approval lead Amir to abandon Hassan at his time of greatest need. This is compounded by his subsequent lies and deception in planting the money and defaming Hassan. Sanaubar is guilty of promiscuity and abandoning her son and husband. Soraya 'sins' against Afghan custom, her guilt made worse by that action coinciding with her mother's stroke.

However, although redemption is possible, it is not easily won. The journey is difficult. Consequently, Amir must leave the comfort of his middle-class existence in America, travel back to the place of his shame, face the deranged Assef, suffer a terrifying and sustained attempt to kill him, endure the subsequent injuries, save and then fail Sohrab, face the reality of Sohrab's suicide attempt, anxiously await news of his survival, struggle to get him entry into the USA and then watch him withdraw into complete silence. This final stage is important, as it is only by returning with Sohrab to America that Amir's redemption is complete, his debt to Hassan paid.

Sanaubar has her face mutilated and Soraya has suffered her father's extreme disappointment and is unable to have children. Their journeys to redemption are also fraught and difficult.

Another important aspect of redemption is the need to confess sins. Amir does this in conversation with Sohrab about Hassan: "I wasn't such a good friend" *(Chapter 23)* and "I couldn't save your father the way he had saved me" *(Chapter 24)*. Sanaubar confesses, "Allah forgive me, I wouldn't even hold you" *(Chapter 16)*, and Soraya admits, "I ran away with an Afghan man [...] We lived together for almost a month" *(Chapter 12)*, speaking their sins aloud as part of their redemption process. Baba, however, remains silent, taking his sins to the grave. It is left to Amir to seek forgiveness on his father's behalf, again in response to Sohrab's questions in Chapter 24. Rahim Khan educates Amir about the importance of forgiveness, emphasising how 'A man who has no conscience, no goodness, does not suffer' *(Chapter 23)* and expressing the hope that he will be able to forgive him, his father, but most importantly himself, framed within God's forgiveness and mercy.

Activity 2

Amir's sin and redemption are linked through the motif of the kite. Write two paragraphs explaining how the kite functions in this way.

Religion

Religion is a source of conflict in the novel given the division that exists between the Sunni and Shi'a branches of Islam.

Within the context of this novel, Ali and Hassan, of the Shi'a branch, are devout and religious, unlike Baba and Amir, who are Sunni Muslims: **'By the time I dragged myself out of bed and lumbered to the bathroom, Hassan had already washed up, prayed the morning *namaz* with Ali, and prepared my breakfast'** *(Chapter 4)*. Godly devotion is one factor contributing to their graceful acceptance of the life they lead and their status in society. Belief offers comfort, enabling them to overcome injustice and discrimination.

Baba, in contrast, presents a different interpretation of religion, living as he does in an urban setting at a time when Kabul was more secular and westernised. He is scathing of the religious clerics, the mullahs, who teach at Amir's school: **"Piss on the beards of all those self-righteous monkeys"** *(Chapter 3)*. His rejection of religious ideology is based on the hypocrisy he sees at the heart of its institutions: **"If there's a God out there, then I would hope he has more important things to attend to than my drinking scotch or eating pork"** *(Chapter 3)*. Amir comments on the contradiction in his father, which means that he *'mocks the story behind this* Eid, *like he mocks everything religious. But he respects the tradition of Eid-e-Qorban' (Chapter 7)*. While the ritual of prayer grates on him, this celebration of how the prophet Ibrahim almost sacrificed his son for God clearly has a personal resonance for Baba given his situation. It also has a practical element to it in that one-third of the meat goes to the poor, a tradition that Baba circumvents by offering up the whole carcass. The symbol of the lamb and the idea of sacrifice contribute strongly to this theme overall.

Baba may reject religious institutions but he does have a strong moral code, which he is keen for Amir to understand, evident in his speech about sin and theft. Aged 12, Amir admits that **'Caught between Baba and the mullahs at school, I still hadn't made up my mind about God'** *(Chapter 7)*. Despite this, on the day of the kite competition, **'when a Koran *ayat* I had learned in my *diniyat* class rose to my lips, I muttered it'** *(Chapter 7)*. This is a pattern that continues, for Amir turns to God, despite his agnosticism, when he desperately wants something. It occurs again when he fears the Russian soldier will shoot Baba and later when Baba's cancer is diagnosed.

More importantly, Amir eventually commits himself fully to God in the wake of Sohrab's attempted suicide. Terrified, as his **'hands are stained with Hassan's blood'**, he prays that **'God doesn't let them get stained with the blood of his boy too'** *(Chapter 25)*. It is a commitment he keeps.

Assef and the Taliban represent the worst of religious intolerance, when extreme 'religious' views are portrayed as a justification for unspeakable cruelty. A Taliban cleric at the soccer match asks, **"How shall we answer those who throw stones at the windows of God's house? WE SHALL THROW THE STONES BACK!"** *(Chapter 21)*.

Moments later, Assef stones a man and woman to death, not for religious ideology but to satisfy his sociopathic tendencies. While emphasising that religion can be divisive, Hosseini also makes clear that the true principles of Islam are still valuable today and much more important in guiding the individual than institutions or groups that dictate specific and twisted interpretations.

Activity 3

a) Find other examples in the novel of the hypocrisy of religious extremism.

b) How do these contrast with instances of genuine faith presented in the novel? Try to find a contrasting occasion for each example you found in part a).

c) Write a summary of Hosseini's attitude to religion as presented in the novel.

Key quotations

I see now that Baba was wrong, there is a God, there always has been. I see Him here, in the eyes of the people in this corridor of desperation [...] There is a God, there has to be, and now I will pray, I will pray that He forgive that I have neglected Him all of these years... *(Chapter 25)*

I prayed morning *namaz* while Soraya slept—I didn't have to consult the prayer pamphlet I had obtained from the mosque anymore; the verses came naturally now, effortlessly. *(Chapter 25)*

Ethnicity

Ethnicity is closely linked with religion and is another source of division. Afghanistan is a very diverse country and its constitution currently mentions 14 different ethnic groups. *The Kite Runner* focuses on the tension between the Pashtuns and Hazaras, and the mistreatment of the latter by the former. The extremism of the Taliban and their mass slaughter of Hazaras at Mazar-i-Sharif in 1998 is the worst that can happen as a result of ethnic tensions. However, the novel depicts that these tensions are ingrained in the people following centuries of prejudice and discrimination. It is taught formally and informally in schools. As a child, Assef 'preaches' it in the street.

Despite their closeness, Baba and Amir never publically recognise Ali and Hassan as their respective friends. Rahim Khan cannot marry his Hazara sweetheart. Some hope, however, is offered in Amir's exchange with General Taheri near the end of the novel. The General's question, "People will ask. They will want to know why there is a Hazara boy living with our daughter. What do I tell them?" receives the following curt reply from Amir, "You will never again refer to him as 'Hazara boy' in my presence. He has a name and it's Sohrab" *(Chapter 25)*. This directly challenges the racism of the older man and suggests that if Afghanistan is to move forward, more people will have to do the same.

Storytelling

The Kite Runner is an example of **metafiction** – a piece of fiction consciously telling a story and deliberately reminding readers of this. Amir reads stories to Hassan as a child, writes stories himself and his eventual profession is as a writer of fiction. The novel contains many stories, both fictional and factual. Soraya shares the story of her past with Amir. Rahim Khan relates the story of Hassan's life since Amir's departure for America. Amir, of course, is the novel's ultimate storyteller.

However, the act of writing fiction and storytelling is not widely accepted as positive. Baba initially dismisses Amir's interest in it: **"But he's always buried in those books or shuffling around the house like he's lost in some dream"** *(Chapter 3)*. General Taheri, when informed that Amir writes fiction, condescendingly states, **"Ah, a storyteller [...] Well, people need stories to divert them at difficult times"** *(Chapter 11)*. His later comment, warning Amir that Soraya must be courted according to traditional Afghan custom, associates fiction and storytelling with another negative – scandalous gossip: **"You see, *everyone* here is a storyteller"** *(Chapter 12)*.

The General's immediate assumption is that Amir writes about history or economics, topics he deems more worthy than mere fiction. This connects with Wahid's question of whether Amir writes about Afghanistan and his encouragement that he does so in order that the world can be informed of their life under the Taliban. Both situations embarrass Amir, who is not capable of facing his own personal history and consequently that of his native country. It is ironic that a man who makes money from the careful expression of words is unable to articulate the most important story of his life. Clearly, Amir is unable to accept reality so fiction is a much more suitable medium for him to work in. Previously, Amir found words and stories to be an escape, initially from his father's coldness but latterly from his secret guilt. This pattern continues into adulthood. He writes fiction because he cannot write about what is real in his own life or what is real about Afghanistan.

With the novel's conclusion, storytelling as a theme becomes entwined with that of Amir's redemption. For example, he is finally able to tell Soraya everything. By seeking forgiveness, reconciling with all things and redeeming himself, Amir can finally face reality, tell the story of his life and that of his country too.

Activity 4

a) What other stories are told in the novel and by whom? What are their purposes?

b) How does Hosseini symbolically represent that Amir is not yet able to read or write about the real world in Chapter 8?

metafiction a piece of fiction consciously telling a story and deliberately reminding readers of this

Abuse of children

Children suffer a range of abuses in this novel. It could be said that Baba is guilty of emotional abuse and neglect of Amir as a child given how he treats him. In failing to identify himself as Hassan's father, he could also be accused of abusing Hassan's right to know his biological father and Amir's right to know his half-brother. Amir also abuses Hassan, particularly his lack of education and loyalty. Hassan suffers further abuse due to his ethnicity from children in the neighbourhood and the soldier who claims to have had sex with his mother.

Most concerning of all, though, is the sexual abuse children suffer throughout the novel at the hands of adults and other children. The rape of Hassan, justified by Assef on the basis of his victim's ethnicity, is deeply shocking and disturbing given that it is perpetrated by one child against another. It causes physical and psychological pain, designed as it is to degrade Hassan. This sexual abuse is not an isolated incident: Kamal becomes a victim of it too and, as the novel reaches its conclusion, Assef, now a Taliban leader, is revealed to be sexually abusing children with no one in a position to stop him. Hosseini places such abuse of children at the heart of his novel. Islam emphasises the importance of raising children with love and compassion, but religious extremism is seen to corrupt these values. Sohrab is presented as a sex slave at the mercy of predatory and deranged Taliban members who embody the grossest hypocrisy.

Hosseini suggests that children suffer the greatest during war. Amir notes on his return to Kabul how 'the beggars were mostly children now, thin and grim-faced, some no older than five or six [...] Hardly any of them sat with an adult male—the wars had made fathers a rare commodity in Afghanistan' *(Chapter 20)*. Worse still is the plight of the children who lived in Baba's orphanage and who lost their lives when it was attacked.

Amir finds that children suffer badly during wartime

The predicament of children, particularly those who do not have wealthy parents, is a depressing and dangerous one. They lose their innocence and their lives. Hosseini uses children as a metaphor for Afghanistan, emphasising how the constant years of political turmoil and violence have ravaged it and stolen its potential. This is encapsulated in Amir's comment about Hassan: **'the face of Afghanistan is that of a boy with a thin-boned frame, a shaved head, and low-set ears, a boy with a Chinese doll face perpetually lit by a harelipped smile'** *(Chapter 4)*. Here, the individual and the human fuses into one with the abstract idea of nationhood.

Key quotation

"Children are fragile, Amir jan. Kabul is already full of broken children and I don't want Sohrab to become another." *(Chapter 17)*

War, honour and pride

The 40-year period in Afghanistan before the overthrow of Zahir Shah by his cousin Daoud was a peaceful one without conflict. Even this act was **'a bloodless coup'** *(Chapter 5)*, although looking back Amir can see that it was also **'the beginning of the end'** *(Chapter 5)* and a new period characterised by war was about to engulf Afghanistan. What follows – the communist *coup d'etat*, Soviet invasion, Afghan–Soviet War, subsequent civil wars, the rise of the Taliban, 9/11 and the West's reaction to that – spans a period from 1973 until 2002 and sees Afghanistan and its people at the mercy of warring factions both within and outside the country.

War and conflict are presented as many things. Capable of igniting overnight, they then endure over decades. They eradicate moral standards, intensifying social and ethnic tensions. What is familiar quickly becomes unfamiliar. War is indiscriminate in its killing; in the novel, it is portrayed primarily as a loss of innocence, expressed allegorically in the rape of Hassan by Assef. This idea is reinforced when essentially good characters like Ali fall victim to the slaughter, the children of Baba's orphanage are blown apart, and Farid's two daughters are killed. The exponents of war display no regard for human life, driven as they are by their own politics and agendas. *Nang* and *namoos* – honour and pride – assume different, less positive interpretations in this context. They certainly do not mean the same as those for which Baba braves death in Chapter 10. However, the very same qualities are required by Amir if he is to rescue Sohrab. It is these values that Baba desperately wanted to instil in Amir and it is these that Amir failed to exhibit in the alleyway all those years ago. By reaching within himself and finding *nang* and *namoos* as

Destruction of buildings in Kabul in the 1990s

an adult, Amir is able to reconcile himself with his father, Hassan and Afghanistan, redeeming himself finally by facing down Assef, rescuing Sohrab and taking him to the USA. Amir's personal war is won but Afghanistan's persisted after the novel's publication. Hosseini clearly questions how different interpretations of honour and pride can reveal the best of Afghanistan but also its worst.

> **Key quotation**
>
> **The generation of Afghan children whose ears would know nothing but the sounds of bombs and gunfire was not yet born.** *(Chapter 5)*

 Activity 5

Write a response arguing for or against the opinion that the novel is ambiguous in its attitude towards violence and war.

Tips for assessment

A theme will permeate the whole novel and any question demanding a response specifically about a theme will require you to range around the whole text to illustrate how it is included and developed. When you are revising a theme, make sure you gather examples from across the novel so you can demonstrate a thorough understanding in your answer.

Masculinity

The novel is concerned with what it means to be male. Baba represents the Afghan notion of manhood: he is physically very powerful, charismatic, successful in business and courageous in the face of danger. Baba is the embodiment of the Pashtun alpha (dominant) male. This is revisited through the story of him fighting a bear, which Amir frequently refers to and dreams about. It is further reinforced through his enjoyment of sports that require physical speed and stamina, such as soccer, or great bravery and horsemanship, such as buzkashi. In his smoking and drinking of scotch, he is not that far removed from the heroes of the western movies that Amir and Hassan enjoy so much. Baba is the man who defends a woman from rape when her own husband is too fearful to do so. His status is such that his sphere of influence extends into Amir's very school, saving him from the corporal punishment administered there.

Unfortunately for Baba, though, Amir does not conform to this stereotype. In fact, he appears to be the opposite of it. Incompetent at soccer, reduced to tears by buzkashi and unable to defend himself in the street, Amir is not what Baba envisaged as a son. In addition, he considers Amir's interest in reading and writing to be feminine, which only alienates Baba further.

Amir's physical and mental weakness is expressed metaphorically through his regular car sickness, which clearly annoys and irritates his father. Baba's opinion of his son changes once they leave Afghanistan, however. In the USA, Baba can appreciate Amir's academic successes. Ironically, as cancer weakens Baba physically, he can appreciate Amir's writing too.

The novel reinforces the idea that masculinity is about courageousness and physical prowess. This is evident in the fact that Amir must display both if he is to redeem himself for his past cowardice and abandonment of Hassan. He is certainly brave to enter the Taliban stronghold and demand Sohrab, exhibiting a new courage by challenging Assef's hypocrisy and sadism: '"What mission is that?" I heard myself say. "Stoning adulterers? Raping children? Flogging women for wearing high heels? Massacring Hazaras? All in the name of Islam?"' *(Chapter 22)*. While he shows little fighting ability, it is enough that Amir withstands the brutal assault by Assef. In doing so, his sins are purged. Consequently, in his dream in Chapter 23, it is Amir now fighting the bear, a symbol that he has reconciled with his father and the Afghan idea of what it means to be a man.

> ### Activity 6
>
> What other forms of masculinity are represented by Ali, Hassan, Rahim Khan and Assef?

Women and motherhood

There is an obvious absence of strong, positive, fully developed female characters in the novel. Although there are exceptions (Amir's mother is a well-respected university lecturer), Afghan society is male dominated and the novel reflects this. A woman's role is often merely functional, such as that of the wet nurse hired to breastfeed Amir and Hassan, or women are seen as a threat to stability and marital harmony as in the case of Sanaubar. Women are further portrayed as impotent and requiring men to rescue them, such as the woman who Baba saves from being raped. Amir's mother, who is presented as highly educated, beautiful and privileged, is dead. Amir grows up in a world devoid of positive females, with the exception of his mother's more benign, indirect influence evident in the books she left behind.

In America, the female characters are slightly more developed, but the theme of their powerlessness continues. Soraya's attempt at independence by moving in with her lover is crushed by her father, who sees that as an affront to his family's honour. His dramatic actions reveal the extent to which an Afghan father will seek to protect honour. His punishment of Soraya is both physical and psychological when he forces her to cut off all of her hair, making it clear that Afghan women do not enjoy the individual freedoms enshrined within America's constitution, even while living there. It is also General Taheri who decides that Amir is suitable to wed his daughter. Soraya has no say in the matter.

Jamila Khan is a further representation of the powerlessness of women, subjected to the will of General Taheri, her interests and opinions suppressed. Overall though, like her daughter, she is positively portrayed as kind and empathetic. More importantly, both characters also offer some hope against this bleak depiction of life for Afghan women. They are active agents in rebelling against the male domination that surrounds them, with Jamila Khan enjoying small private victories and Soraya quite significant ones. In this more positive context, these women represent Afghanistan: waiting, enduring and capable of rising again when their oppressors have given up or been worn down.

The women in the novel also reflect the idea of motherhood, but once again this is less than positive. Giving birth kills Amir's mother. Sanaubar no sooner gives birth than she publically rejects Hassan and maternal responsibility. Soraya's desperate attempts to be a mother are foiled by her infertility, leaving Jamila Khan alone to portray a more positive representation of motherhood.

Key quotations

"I didn't tell you," Soraya said, dabbing at her eyes, "but my father showed up with a gun that night. He told… him… that he had two bullets in the chamber, one for him [her lover] and one for himself if I didn't come home." *(Chapter 13)*

Maybe it was because I had been raised by men; I hadn't grown up around women and had never been exposed firsthand to the double standard with which Afghan society sometimes treated them. *(Chapter 13)*

"While you're busy knitting sweaters, my dear, I have to deal with the community's perception of our family." *(Chapter 25)*

 Activity 7

In what ways are the mothers in the novel able to triumph?

Friendship

The novel depicts how social and ethnic divisions make friendships difficult. Baba's friendship with Rahim Khan is one of the strongest in the novel but they are from the same religious and ethnic group, bonded further by the same business interests. Friendship is explored most in the relationships of Baba and Ali, and Amir and Hassan. The latter is a reflection of the former, even presenting Baba and Amir as the initiators of childhood mischief. A clear picture of friendship is portrayed across the generations, and yet there is also an acute sense of division and of lines that are not to be crossed.

For all the friendship that exists, it is never openly acknowledged – 'in none of his stories did Baba ever refer to Ali as his friend' – and similarly Amir 'never thought of Hassan and me [Amir] as friends either' *(Chapter 4)*. If this is an unspoken reality, Assef addresses it more explicitly and cruelly in Chapter 7, scornfully mocking Hassan's assertion that he and Amir are friends: '"Friends?" Assef said, laughing. "You pathetic fool! Someday you'll wake up from your little fantasy and learn just how good of a friend he is"' *(Chapter 7)*. Unknown to Assef, his words are prophetic, for it is that very day that Amir betrays Hassan. What follows is far from friendship. First, Amir tries to encourage his father to get rid of Ali and Hassan. Then he assaults Hassan with pomegranates and afterwards frames him as a thief.

Juxtaposed with this is Hassan's unconditional love and friendship for Amir. He offers moral support to the anxious Amir on the day of the kite competition. Hassan encourages the would-be-writer with words of praise. He sacrifices himself in the most selfless way imaginable to ensure the last kite is secured for Amir and, despite knowing that he was abandoned and has had his good name denigrated by Amir, he later accepts a guilt that is not his. Nor does time dilute Hassan's love for Amir. Hassan signs off his letter to Amir by assuring him that should he return to Kabul, he **'will find an old faithful friend waiting'** *(Chapter 17)*. How much of Hassan's loyalty is based on social inequalities and Hassan's understanding of his role and place in society is unclear, but the resolution of the conflict at the heart of their relationship is complicated by the revelation that Baba fathered Hassan. Amir is reluctant to accept the challenge presented by Rahim Khan initially, so much so that the older man resorts to blackmailing Amir emotionally by presenting the request as that of a dying man's last wish. It is only with the revelation that Hassan is his half-brother and after much thought that Amir agrees to accept the challenge. This means that Amir is acting in defence of his own flesh and blood, not a friend.

Activity 8

Write a paragraph analysing how the pomegranate tree, kites and the *Shahnamah* each contribute to the theme of friendship between Amir and Hassan.

Activity 9

How does the relationship between Assef, Kamal and Wali contribute to the theme of friendship?

Immigration

There has always been a tradition of Afghan people moving within the country and also out of it, long before the Soviet invasion in 1979. Certainly the issue of immigration became much more pressing from this point onwards. The ebb and flow of politics and conflict means that ethnic groups, once safe, can quickly become more vulnerable. *The Kite Runner* deals in most detail with the movement of upper middle-class Pashtuns into America in the early 1980s; they had the money to flee as the communists tightened their grip. Baba and Amir's escape is described as an act of stealth: **'You couldn't trust anyone in Kabul anymore'** *(Chapter 10)*. Their passage to Islamabad, into Peshawar and finally the USA takes some six months. It is an expensive journey filled with danger and uncertainty, with the refugees' fate in the hands of unscrupulous people smugglers like Karim. Baba, Amir and the Taheri family arrive safely, but others like Kamal and his father do not.

America is a place where the younger generation of Afghans settle quicker than their older relations. General Taheri's migraines, Khala Jamila's stroke and Baba's cancer symbolise that they are unsuited to life in the USA. Baba's violent outburst in the Nguyens' grocery store is one example of his inability to manage the cultural differences. What he sees as an assault on his honesty and integrity is simply one family-run business protecting itself from basic fraud. It is difficult to underestimate the challenge facing this older generation. In Kabul, Baba is well known, highly successful, respected and lives a life of comfort. The USA, however, means many hours of hard, physical labour, a modest apartment and the absence of cherished old friends. General Taheri has given up the status of a position in government for welfare cheques and social anonymity. In this world, a former Afghan surgeon now runs a hot dog stand. Consequently, it is no surprise that these refugees gravitate towards each other, congregating in the market in San Jose where they speak their own languages, play Afghan music, talk politics, prepare and eat Afghan food, and converse about mutual friends. This Afghan community, away from Afghanistan, offers security, familiarity and comfort.

The novel's conclusion reinforces this when the Afghan community gathers to celebrate its New Year and soon **'A half-dozen kites were flying high, speckles of bright yellow, red, and green against the gray sky'** *(Chapter 25)*. It creates issues for the younger generation of Afghans, caught between the liberal western view of the world and the much more socially conservative traditions of Afghanistan. Soraya suffers most in this regard when her elopement is quickly and decisively quashed by her father. Yet the 'scandal' follows her from Virginia as the Afghan community gossips about her past.

Amir is victim of it too. Baba warns him, sensing his initial interest in Soraya, that things must be done the Afghan way despite being in the USA: **"Remember this [...] The man [General Taheri] is a Pashtun to the root. He has *nang* and *namoos* [...] Just don't embarrass me, that's all I ask"** *(Chapter 12)*. It is wise advice, for only by showing due respect and then approaching the General in the traditional Afghan way does Amir have any chance of gaining Soraya's hand in marriage. Even then he needs to have the right family background as well.

America is a place where the Afghan community can thrive, albeit while retaining strong links to the country and traditions left behind. Amir becomes a professional writer and Soraya a high school teacher. Her uncle Sharif works for the Immigration and Naturalisation Service. The theme of immigration returns powerfully at the novel's conclusion as Amir tries desperately to adopt Sohrab and bring him back to the USA. Bureaucracy and lawlessness means that this is virtually impossible. It is Uncle Sharif, an immigrant himself, who outlines the way that Amir can secure Sohrab's future in the USA.

Key quotations

What was I doing on this road in the middle of the night? I should have been in bed, under my blanket, a book with dog-eared pages at my side. This had to be a dream. Had to be. Tomorrow morning, I'd wake up, peek out the window: No grim-faced Russian soldiers patrolling the sidewalks, no tanks rolling up and down the streets of my city... *(Chapter 10)*

He missed people milling in and out of his house, missed walking down the bustling aisles of Shor Bazaar and greeting people who knew him and his father, knew his grandfather, people who shared ancestors with him, whose pasts intertwined with his. *(Chapter 11)*

...you need the cooperation of the child's country of origin. Now, that's difficult under the best of circumstances, and, to quote you, this *is* Afghanistan [...] That makes things extremely complicated. Just about impossible. *(Chapter 24)*

Activity 10

How does Hosseini present immigration as both a negative and positive thing in the novel?

Loyalty and lies

Loyalty is one of a number of important qualities necessary in a good friendship. Ali demonstrates loyalty to Baba, but Hassan's loyalty to Amir takes this quality to new degrees of purity and perfection. The extent to which this is derived from his social status and position of servitude remains open to debate, for he is essentially Amir's servant as the two boys grow up. There is also the reality that Amir's grandfather saved the orphaned Ali from a probable life of destitution, embedding further layers of debt and gratitude in the servant and his son.

It is Amir who makes the idea of loyalty explicit when he challenges Hassan's loyalty to him with the question about whether or not he would eat dirt if he asked him to. It is a spontaneous question, not like the later premeditated attack with the pomegranates, but its motives are questionable, designed as it is to **'toy'** *(Chapter 6)* with Hassan. Amir admits his intention is to be **'cruel'** *(Chapter 6)*. The question clearly disturbs Hassan, who not only answers as required in the affirmative but issues his own challenge in response, **"Would you ever ask me to do such a thing, Amir agha?"** *(Chapter 6)*. Amir sees this as a test of his honesty and confidently asserts that Hassan believes his response that he would never ask such a thing of him. Hassan, however, is described as having searched Amir's face **'for a long time'** before answering *(Chapter 6)*. This suggests a certain caution about Amir's motives and uncertainty about how to respond. In a later episode, Amir confesses how Hassan **'was always doing that, reading my mind'** *(Chapter 6)*. In light of this comment, his earlier confidence about concealing the truth from Hassan is misplaced. If Hassan has an idea that Amir is neither honest nor loyal, then his many selfless actions are all the more impressive. Amir's disloyalty is also doubly ironic. He contextualises his abandonment of Hassan in the alley as a bid to gain Baba's approval and affection. However, his betrayal of Hassan is a disloyalty to Baba too. Firstly, it betrays Baba's principles of honour and pride, which he holds so dear and desperately wishes Amir would exemplify. Secondly, although unknown to Amir at the time, it is a betrayal of his own flesh and blood, something that would anger Baba even more. These wrongs are righted by the novel's conclusion when Amir's loyalty saves Sohrab, his nephew. This satisfies the betrayal of blood years before and also upholds his father's principles. Finally, by being loyal to family and principle, Amir finds reconciliation and redemption.

 Activity 11

Find others examples of when Hassan is portrayed as understanding Amir and his thinking.

Writing about themes

A question specifically about a theme might seem straightforward, but it can be easy to stray into simple storytelling or to veer off the point of the question. Your answer should reveal *how* a theme is developed through the writer's use of character, language, symbolism, form and structure. Tracking this development and making links across the text will help you demonstrate how an idea is introduced, then repeated and expanded as the story progresses.

Structural ideas such as contrast can help you get started when discussing a theme. For example, a question might ask you to discuss how Hosseini contrasts Hassan's loyalty with Amir's disloyalty. This could lead into a discussion of the theme of friendship and how true friendship is demonstrated – or lacking – within the novel. This could then be underpinned by analysis of how the motifs of the kite and the pomegranate tree contribute to these themes. Other relationships could then be explored, such as those of Baba and Ali, and of Baba and Rahim Khan.

Readers' responses to a literary text are influenced by their own experiences and opinions and the values they hold. These significantly shape how a text is read, what is focused on and how it is interpreted. As a result, there is never a definitive reading of a novel, and your own interpretation should be informed by a variety of critical approaches to the text you are studying. Knowing and appreciating these enriches your own approach.

Marxist criticism

Marxist criticism is based on the thoughts and ideas of Karl Marx (1818–83), a philosopher, economist, sociologist and revolutionary socialist who greatly influenced modern political and economic thinking. Marx argued that a capitalist society is essentially hierarchical and only through class conflict and revolution could it be challenged and overcome. He believed that those at the top, the bourgeoisie (the wealthy upper middle class), control the means of production, exploiting those at the bottom, the proletariat (the working class), for their labour in order to make money. Maintaining this system is in the vested interests of the bourgeoisie as it ensures that power and wealth stay in their hands. Marx argued that the proletariat or working class needs to revolt and overthrow the ruling class in order to create a more equitable society in which wealth and power is evenly distributed – in effect a communist society.

In *The Kite Runner*, the divisions between the social classes are intensified by ethnic and religious ones. Consequently, the upper middle class are Pashtun and Sunni while the lower class are Hazara and Shi'a. This is exemplified through the master/servant relationships of Baba and Amir with Ali and Hassan.

Baba's house is 'the most beautiful' in the Wazir Akbar Khan district, which in turn is 'a new and affluent neighbohood' in Kabul *(Chapter 2)*. Contrast this with 'the modest little mud hut' *(Chapter 2)* that is home to Ali and Hassan. Baba's home is lavish and plush. There are 'Intricate mosaic tiles [...] Gold-stitched tapestries [...] a crystal chandelier' *(Chapter 2)* in juxtaposition to the humble possessions and decorations of Ali's home, described as 'spare, clean, dimly lit by a pair of kerosene lamps. There were two mattresses on opposite sides of the room [...] a three-legged stool, and a wooden table in the corner' *(Chapter 2)*.

Amir grows up with a life of privilege, Hassan as a servant

The difference could not be clearer. Baba's house is situated in one of the most upmarket areas of Kabul, so much so that it attracts the Taliban, who later choose to settle there. However, Ali and Hassan's home, following their departure from Kabul, is in an incredibly impoverished area. Now living in a village outside Bamiyan, where many of the Hazara were concentrated, Hassan is found by Rahim Khan to be in **'not much more than a glorified hut'** among a **'cluster of mud houses'** in the middle of a **'barren land'** *(Chapter 16)*. The Hazaras, following many years of marginalisation, live in third-world conditions while their Pashtun Sunni masters live in luxury and splendour, something Marxist critics would strongly oppose.

Marxist readers of the text also note the very different lifestyles of both groups and their attitudes towards religion. Baba drinks alcohol, smokes and throws lavish parties. He becomes **'one of the richest merchants in Kabul'** *(Chapter 3)*, generating an income that allows him to drive an imported car, fly **'to Tehran for a month to watch the World Cup games on television'** *(Chapter 3)* and build an orphanage, **'paying for the engineers, electricians, plumbers, and laborers, not to mention the city officials'** *(Chapter 3)* himself. He has a degree of wealth, privilege and influence within the community that Ali and Hassan can never achieve. When he speaks disparagingly about the mullahs, he does so safe in the knowledge that he is immune from their punishment.

On the other hand, Hassan's subjugation and lower-class status is so ingrained that, on returning to Kabul with Rahim Khan and Farzana, he still chooses to live in the hut that was his former home rather than accept the offer to live in the main house. The social, economic and political systems of the time are designed to ensure that this situation will never change. Ali and Hassan's routine revolves around their daily chores and prayers. Their religious devotion may offer comfort and spiritual fulfilment but is also seen more negatively by Marxist critics as a way of enslaving them further, rendering them too passive, too accepting of their circumstances and too willing to forgive the abuses they suffer.

Linked powerfully to this is their lack of education, which disempowers them even further. The *Shahnamah* presented to Amir on his 13th birthday by Ali and Hassan, is a book neither could read. Illiteracy keeps the Hazara people ignorant, unable to identify and articulate their grievances and dependent on religion, so of no risk to the established Pashtun order. Amir's easy and gratuitous manipulation of Hassan by teaching him that 'imbecile' means 'intelligent' stands as a very powerful metaphor for the manipulation of the lower class by the more dominant one.

Social and political structures such as these have been established for centuries and are so etched into the psychology of the dispossessed (who have had power taken away from them) that breaking them becomes impossible. The casual racism and sectarianism depicted within the novel is a manifestation of this. It enables the powerful to justify their mistreatment of others on the grounds of their superiority.

The massacre at Mazar-i-Sharif is the endpoint of such views. The Hazaras ultimately are trapped in a continual cycle of disempowerment, which pervades all aspects of their lives and offers little hope of change. Hassan's statement to Amir – **"I *like* where I live"** *(Chapter 6)* – makes this clear.

Activity 1

a) How far do you agree with the idea that Ali and Hassan are enslaved by their religion?

b) What evidence can you find to support or refute this idea within the novel?

Tips for assessment

Upgrade

Literature, by its very nature, is open to interpretation. While it is important that you appreciate the different ways in which critics have responded to the novel, the examiner is most interested in how you use this knowledge to inform your own interpretation.

An interesting point from a Marxist perspective is the Saur Revolution, which brought the republic to an end and the Communist People's Democratic Party of Afghanistan to power in 1978. It was this, along with the subsequent Soviet invasion in 1979, that made Baba and Amir flee the country to avoid being targeted because of their wealth. Assef's family remains in Afghanistan but quickly becomes a victim of the new regime. He comments on their intention to **'Round up the rich, throw them in jail, make an example for the comrades'** *(Chapter 22)*. This was, theoretically, an attempt to begin the Marxist process of redistributing wealth and power more fairly. However, this process only ever served to concentrate power and wealth in the hands of a new elite, and the working class only swapped one form of oppression and subjugation for another.

Key quotation

...everyone knew the communists had no class. They came from poor families with no name. The same dogs who weren't fit to lick my shoes before the *Shorawi* came were now ordering me at gunpoint, *Parchami* flag on their lapels, making their little point about the fall of the bourgeoisie and acting like they were the ones with class. *(Chapter 22)*

Activity 2

To what extent do you believe that the novel presents the period before the overthrow of Zahir Shah in 1973 as a golden age in Afghanistan?

Amir as Afghanistan

Another critical interpretation sees Amir as representing the country of Afghanistan. For example, the country has a large number of ethnic groups and tensions exist between them. There is also the religious divide of Sunni and Shi'a Islam as well. The conflict within Amir about the nature of his relationship with Hassan and his assertion that they are not friends, even though they behave as such, reflects the reality within the country. Amir is conflicted, just as the country is. Other parallels exist; for example, Afghanistan is a patriarchal society, with men completely dominant and most women subservient to their wishes. In the novel, Amir's mother is dead; this could be interpreted as the absence of matriarchal influence in the country. Afghanistan has witnessed and been torn apart by decades of war, which has prevented its economic growth and prosperity. In the same way, Amir witnesses the rape of Hassan, is consequently tortured by his own inaction, and his psychological and emotional development is stunted as a result. Moreover, if a new and successful Afghanistan is to emerge, one that can participate fully in and contribute positively to affairs in the region, much violence and suffering will have to be endured, just as Amir had to withstand and endure the vicious assault by Assef in order to gain his redemption.

Activity 3

In what other ways can Amir be said to represent Afghanistan?

Activity 4

a) Research three or four online reviews of the novel. What are these reviews positive and negative about?

b) Write a short response to each, presenting the opposite view to the critic.

Psychoanalytic criticism

Psychoanalytic interpretations of text are based on the work of Sigmund Freud (1856–1939), an Austrian neurologist who developed psychoanalysis (the use of dialogue between doctor and patient) to understand better deeply rooted and complex reasons for human behaviour. He put forward the controversial theory of psychosexual development, which outlined five stages through which a human must pass in order to develop and mature fully.

Freud suggested that failure to complete one of these stages or to miss one out completely runs the risk of the maturation process becoming stuck. Consequently, although someone might be an adult in years, psychologically and emotionally they could be stuck in a childhood stage of development due to experiencing a traumatic event or because their needs at that stage were not met or were met excessively.

Each stage centres on a specific part of the human body.

- Oral (the mouth): age 0–1, when infants learn to suck milk and swallow
- Anal (the anus): age 1–3, when toddlers learn to use the toilet
- Phallic (the penis/clitoris): age 3–5/6, when young children become aware of anatomical differences between male and female and experience emotional conflict
- Latent (none): age 5/6 to puberty, when children concentrate on school, hobbies and friendship rather than sexual development
- Genital (the penis/vagina): from puberty to adulthood, when teenagers experiment sexually and eventually settle in a loving relationship.

Freud believed that an adult's behaviour could be explained by understanding the impact of such events in their childhood, which they subsequently buried deep in their subconscious. He argued that these negative and repressed memories and emotions do not leave the individual unless they are identified, talked through and fully understood. If not, the individual fails to develop and their actions become repeated in adulthood as a way of avoiding certain realities or as a method of self-punishment. Dreams are important in psychoanalysis as they often relate to the repressed feelings and emotions of the individual and act as a manifestation of these.

Psychoanalytic critics of the novel focus much of their attention on Amir's failure to help Hassan in the alleyway. This can also be explained through Freud's idea that the human mind has three distinct parts – the id, the ego and the super ego.

- The id is the part that tells you to do whatever you want, whenever you want, in order to satisfy your basic instincts.
- The ego tries to modify the id, rationalising why it may not be a good idea simply to do what you want when you want.
- The super ego acts like a conscience, emphasising how your actions relate to society's rules, expectations and norms. In many respects it is the ideal self.

During the terrifying moment of Assef's assault on Hassan in Chapter 7, Amir is dominated by the id. His instincts are to protect himself even though his ego is telling him that Hassan needs help and his super ego is telling him that Assef's actions are immoral and his own inaction is wrong. At first Amir is gripped by terror: **'I felt paralyzed'**. Then he attempts to block out the horror before him by desperately and childishly wishing it away: **'Shut my eyes'**. Finally he flees: **'In the end, I ran'** (Chapter 7).

Activity 5

a) Research Freud's theory of psychosexual development and its five stages further.

b) To what extent does Hosseini use the five Freudian stages of psychosexual development in his characterisation of Amir?

Given how traumatic the rape is for Amir and the extent to which it plagues his subsequent life, psychoanalyst critics would argue that it results in Amir failing to move on to the next stage in his psychosexual development, thus preventing him from becoming a fully functioning adult. Although Amir's life has been shaken by trauma previously through the death of his mother, it could be argued that he is able to pass from the first stage (the oral stage of Freud's theory) because of the wet nurse hired by his father. However, Amir is unable to pass through the third (phallic) stage and the important Oedipus complex experience of his growing up. In this theory, Freud proposes that a male child must unconsciously undergo a feeling of competition with his father for the affections of his mother. (The theory derives its name from the story of Oedipus from Greek **mythology**, who unwittingly killed his father and married his mother.) Given that Amir's mother is dead, this stage of his development and the processing of these emotions is not possible. Another significant experience, which follows the Oedipal one, is when the boy moves beyond the feeling of competition with his father to when he desires to bond with his father instead and develop the same masculine qualities. Amir is also denied this in his childhood, as his father is cold and removed, and so obviously disappointed by Amir's lack of courage and physical prowess.

Activity 6

a) To what extent could Rahim Khan be considered a substitute mother for Amir?

b) How would this affect a psychoanalytical interpretation of whether Amir passes through the third stage of Freud's theory?

A psychoanalytical reading of the text would look very closely at the dreams within the novel too. Clearly Amir's dreams about Baba fighting the bear relate to Amir's deep concerns about his father's masculine traits of strength, bravery and courage, and his own lack of these. The dreams reinforce his feelings of inferiority and rejection. However, when Amir stands up to Assef, suffers the beating and leaves with Sohrab, this dream returns. But this time he is the man fighting the bear. This represents that he has finally demonstrated the qualities of his father and in doing so reconciled with him. His repressed thoughts give comfort here. Similarly, during Assef's rape of Hassan, the fractured workings of Amir's mind are reflected in the narrative being disrupted by two memories and a dream. The latter is loaded with significance for Amir.

mythology the study of ancient tales and stories relating to a specific religion or culture

In the dream, it is winter, his favourite season, but he is lost. His cries for help are drowned out by the wind, emphasising his increasing desperation and anxiety as the attack continues on Hassan. His footprints disappear in the falling snow, suggesting that he is being erased from the landscape and life, a reflection of his cowardice, which renders him useless in a land like Afghanistan. Overpowered and weak, he is knocked to the ground, which again reflects his lack of masculinity and physical strength. His saviour is **'A familiar shape'** *(Chapter 7)*, who is clearly Hassan, and whose palm is cut and drips blood on the snow, just as it will after Assef's assault.

As their hands touch, the weather is transformed and Amir is *'in a field of apple green grass' (Chapter 7)*. Overhead, *'the clear sky is filled with kites, green, yellow, red, orange' (Chapter 7)*. This emphasises Hassan's role as Amir's frequent saviour, making Amir's current betrayal all the more terrible. The landscape described here echoes that of the two boys under the pomegranate tree, a symbol of their friendship. The colourful kites filling the sky symbolise their friendship and a happier, more innocent childhood time. Tellingly, there is no blue kite in the dream – the colour of the kite that Hassan retrieved for Amir.

Activity 7

Hassan undergoes a terrible ordeal as a child. Map his development using the psychosexual developmental stages. Why do you think Hassan is able to fully mature despite the traumas he suffers?

Feminist criticism

When reading a text, feminist critics focus their attention on the ways in which women are portrayed and their place within a patriarchal society. Particular scrutiny is paid to how women are treated by men, how they interact with each other, and the extent to which they are free and empowered. Indeed, the idea exists of a specifically female form of writing – *ecriture feminine*– and in its non-linear narrative and use of more than one narrative voice, it could be said that *The Kite Runner* exemplifies some of its characteristics. However, in its portrayal of women, the novel is seen by many critics to be **misogynistic**.

None of the women in the novel has any power; it is all held in the hands of men. Amir's mother is portrayed as perfect: she was highly intelligent, virtuous, very beautiful and even connected to Afghan royalty, but she is also dead, so her influence on events is limited. Another early female presence is the wet nurse hired to breastfeed Amir and Hassan. This again would anger feminists and be seen as a man reducing the mothering role to a basic commercial transaction.

Sanaubar is also depicted in a negative way. She is clearly a very attractive and sensual woman, but her beauty is portrayed as a threat to the established male order. Rather than condemning the men who succumb to her sexual allure, she is often presented as the problem and the men as mere victims. It is **'Sanaubar's** brilliant green eyes and impish face' that 'tempted countless men into sin' *(Chapter 2)*. This antagonises feminist readers of the text as blame lies with the woman when the men are culpable too. Sanaubar is also depicted as insensitive and uncaring. She has contempt for Ali and 'made no secret of her disdain for his appearance' *(Chapter 2)*. Worse still is her instant, scornful rejection of the newly born Hassan. The news that Baba is Hassan's father cannot save her from readers' disgust at her actions. Although the infant came out 'smiling', Sanaubar is said to have 'seen the cleft lip, and barked a bitter laugh' and 'refused to even hold Hassan, and just five days later, she was gone' *(Chapter 2)*.

Sanaubar's sudden return continues the misogynistic treatment of women. Dressed in a burqa, she now wears a Taliban-imposed garment, which covers all aspects of her woman's body, including her eyes. Designed to ensure modesty by covering the female form, it is sometimes seen by feminists as another gross affront to a woman's rights. Sanaubar has also been on the receiving end of some rough treatment, no doubt at the hands of men, as the scars on her face suggest she has been attacked and punished for her notorious beauty.

Some feminists see the burqa as an affront to women's rights

In America, the two main female characters are Jamila Khan and Soraya. While both are more substantial, neither is fully developed and both remain disempowered. Jamila Khan is subjugated to the wishes of her husband, General Taheri. His word is law, reflecting the traditional Afghan husband. Their marriage is conditional on her giving up singing, which the General considered low class. By the time they arrive in the USA, their marriage appears to be quite loveless, as the General's pettiness is enough to make her cry and they sleep apart. Even her tendency to hypochondria, understandable in someone who has suffered a stroke, is mocked by her husband. In America, he continues to rule her life. Her wish to sing one song at her daughter's wedding is overruled: 'the general gave her one of his looks and the matter was buried' *(Chapter 13)*. She is portrayed as kindly, but because she knows and accepts her place, feminist critics would question her portrayal. Amir depicts a quiet if unexciting and unfulfilling existence: 'Khala Jamila played the lotto once a week and watched Johnny Carson every night. She spent her days in the garden' *(Chapter 13)*. Her love for Amir is founded upon the fact that he 'had relieved her of the greatest fear of every Afghan mother: that no honourable *khastegar*

misogynistic prejudiced against women

would ask for her daughter's hand. That her daughter would age alone, husbandless, childless' *(Chapter 13)*. Amir is presented as the hero in a fairy tale, who is not just Soraya's but also her mother's saviour. This reveals the extent to which Afghan culture in the novel completely marginalises and disempowers females.

Soraya is also very much a victim of this. Her attempt at freedom by eloping at the age of 18 to live with a man brings shame upon her father and her family. General Taheri's violent and threatening behaviour is designed to terrify her lover, emotionally blackmail his daughter and ensure he gets his own way – which he does. A further painful reality is how the women of the immigrant Afghan community in the novel are complicit in spreading gossip about her situation; there is no sense of sisterhood. Soraya seems regretful about her actions by the time she meets Amir, but she is stuck in a difficult situation, balancing the freedoms she observes her college friends enjoying and the iron rule of her father at home. Her frustrations are clear as she rails against the hypocrisy of male Afghan culture and her father's preference for her to become a lawyer rather than a teacher, albeit not in her father's presence.

More positively, feminists would argue, Soraya does rebel against the patriarchal order by becoming a teacher against her father's wishes. She also enjoys a more important victory when her father, slowly relenting with time and weakening with age after an injury, **'sometimes [...] sat in on some of her classes [...] Sometimes he even took notes'** *(Chapter 14)*.

Activity 8

a) How does Khala Jamila rebel against the General's authority in Chapter 14?

b) In what ways does Amir's visit to the American Embassy in Chapter 24 portray a patriarchal society?

c) How would a feminist critic respond to the portrayal of Farzana?

Postcolonial criticism

Colonialism refers to the domination of countries in Africa, Asia and Latin America by European superpowers including England, France, Spain and Portugal during an era stretching from the 15th to the early 20th centuries. Having overpowered the countries on these continents, the Europeans set about making money from their resources and native labour to develop their own wealth and expand their empires. Postcolonial literature is the relatively recent body of work that has arisen out of these previously colonised countries since they gained independence. While in power the colonising countries had controlled all discourse and portrayed themselves positively and those they colonised negatively. For example, the native peoples were often presented as uneducated, unintelligent and unchristian savages and their subjugation was presented as an opportunity to become civilised. This was clearly designed to mask the real intentions of these countries: the exploitation of weaker nations. However, postcolonial literature challenges the historical portrayal of the native peoples and presents a clearer picture of life in these colonised countries.

Postcolonial writers consider a number of issues, including how the identity of the colonised is misrepresented by the coloniser and what the true identity is; how the formerly colonised can reclaim control of their language, traditions, culture and heritage; the relationship between the coloniser and the colonised once independence has been gained, and also the relationship between those who remained during the period of colonisation and those who left the country. Postcolonial literature embraces the work of immigrants who write about these issues too. A key work in this area is Edward Said's *Orientalism* (1978), which is highly critical of the West's view of things and challenges its view of the East as inaccurate, condescending, stereotypical and ignorant. Essentially, Said argues that we understand the East through what the West tells us to think and believe. Indeed, postcolonial literature goes further by criticising those natives who came to power after independence by claiming that they implemented western designs, policies and practices that continue to harm their own countries to this day.

The Kite Runner clearly fits into this framework, with Hosseini writing about his native country as an Afghan immigrant living in the USA – just like his narrator. Most Americans and citizens of western countries were introduced to and understand Afghanistan through the media in light of the 9/11 attacks. As Afghanistan was under the control of the Taliban and harbouring Osama bin Laden and Al-Qaeda, such coverage was almost universally negative. Amir comments on how American patriotism mushroomed and 'The American flag suddenly appeared everywhere' *(Chapter 25)* as Americans absorbed all that was said in the media. This depicted Afghanistan as home to bloodthirsty zealots determined to destroy the USA and its citizens. It became the topic of conversation for 'people sipping lattes at Starbucks' *(Chapter 25)* and public opinion unconditionally supported the US-led coalition's trillion-dollar 'War on Terror'.

Hosseini, however, challenges this narrative through his novel and offers a glimpse into an alternative Afghanistan, not biased and filtered through a western lens. This is the gentle, loving and forgiving Afghanistan of Ali and Hassan. It is the business acumen of Baba, which hints at how that nation could prosper if free of war and conflict. It is the warmth and hospitality of Wahid, the bravery of Farzana, the culture and intelligence of Amir's mother, and the professor reduced to begging on the streets of Kabul. It is the courage of Baba faced with a drunken armed soldier intent on evil, the humanity and vision of Rahim Khan, who knows how to bring an end to a cycle of lies and the damage it has caused to three generations. Hosseini invites readers to speak and learn Afghan languages, celebrate its customs and traditions, and enjoy the country's landscape. His book celebrates the best of Afghanistan while the West has been broadcasting the worst.

The novel also examines the lives of the Afghans who have settled in the USA, portraying a group of families greatly reduced in status but alive and adjusting to the significant challenges such a move demands. This allows readers to observe the different ways the characters manage their situations, some more successfully than others. Above all, members of the Afghan community are presented as creating a home from home, coming together to live the Afghan way as far as America will let them.

Amir's return to the country of his birth allows comparison of the 'Little Afghanistan' of California with the reality of life for those who did not leave. He is ridiculed by Farid for his belief that he is an Afghan. Assef also questions what he sees as Amir's abandonment of the country.

This creates problems for Amir and Hosseini within a postcolonial reading of the text. Is the novel a true reflection of Afghanistan, given that it has been written by a man who has become westernised through his education, employment and the opportunities America has offered him? Would someone else be better suited to reveal the true Afghanistan, someone who never left it? That may be so, but certainly Hosseini's novel offers a very significant view of what Afghanistan really is, to balance and challenge the presentation of Afghanistan in the western media.

> **Key quotations**
>
> "You've *always* been a tourist here [Afghanistan], you just didn't know it." *(Chapter 19)*
>
> "What are you doing with that whore [America]? Why aren't you here, with your Muslim brothers, serving your country?" *(Chapter 22)*

> **Activity 9**
>
> Which character from the novel do you think is best placed to tell the real story of Afghanistan?

Different interpretations within the text

Demonstrating the ability to make an informed interpretation of the novel at whole-text level is very important. However, you should also demonstrate how, within the text, there are sentences and passages that are open to interpretation, not at the level of Marxist, feminist, postcolonial or psychoanalytic debate, but more simply as a result of the richness of Hosseini's writing. Exploiting these opportunities will make clear to the examiner that you are a close and engaged reader of text.

For example, while fleeing the rape in the alley, Amir comments on how he was weeping and still biting down on his fist **'hard enough to draw blood'** *(Chapter 7)*. On one level, his tears are an emotional reaction to what he has just seen, while the physical pain he is inflicting upon himself is an attempt to manage those feelings and not become completely overwhelmed by them. The fact that he bites himself and draws blood emphasises how hard this is to control. However, it also reflects Hassan's situation as the victim of a sexual assault that causes extreme physical and emotional pain. Not only is Hosseini skilfully reflecting the nature of the attack, while avoiding the need to be explicit about it, but he is also strongly aligning Amir with Hassan at this key moment in the novel. This prepares readers for the reality that Hassan will never leave Amir, despite Amir's rejection, lies and physical escape from him into America.

Activity 10

Discuss the possible interpretations of the following quotation. Mr Fayyaz, the manager of the hotel in Islamabad where Amir and Sohrab stay, tells Amir:

"The thing about you Afghanis is that... well, you people are a little reckless."
(Chapter 24)

Writing about critical views

Questions that ask you to consider the novel from a specific interpretation do not require you to focus solely on that one critical approach. You can argue that an alternative interpretation is more appropriate if you wish. In such a situation, it is advisable that you first make clear your understanding of why some critics believe the novel is best interpreted from the view proposed in the question before moving on to discuss your favoured option in greater detail.

It can be useful during revision to practise writing responses to challenge critical views, even if you might agree with them. Considering the counter-arguments to a view will make you think more carefully about an argument's credibility and ultimately help you to write a stronger response.

Exam skills

Knowing your course

It is important to know why you are reading *The Kite Runner* and how you will be tested on it.

Activity 1

Answer these questions without looking at your notes or handouts. If you are unsure about any of them, make sure you check!

a) Are you reading *The Kite Runner* in order to do a coursework or exam response?

b) If it is for an exam response:

- Will you have a clean copy of the novel to use during the exam?

- How much time do you have to complete the whole exam?

- How much time do you have to answer the question on *The Kite Runner*?

- How will you divide up this time in terms of choosing a question, planning and writing your response?

- Is the question on *The Kite Runner* worth the same marks as the other questions you have to answer?

- Will you have a choice of questions and have to select one?

- Will you have an option to base your response on an extract from the novel?

- Will you have to write a response that links *The Kite Runner* with another novel or novels?

c) If it is for a coursework response:

- When is your deadline?

- How many words must you write?

- Will you get some feedback and be able to work on improving your first draft?

- How many marks is your response worth?

- Will you have to select a question from a list provided by your teacher or create your own?

- Will you have to link *The Kite Runner* with another novel or novels?

d) Have you read and understood the mark scheme used to assess your exam or coursework question?

Selecting the right question

Success in the exam requires a clear strategy. It is important that you know how long you have and how your time should be divided between the questions. It is also a good idea to be clear about how you will organise the time for each specific question in terms of choosing it, planning your response and then writing it.

The next challenge is to select the right question, if you have a choice. You should read the questions carefully and underline the key words in each so that you fully understand what each demands. Then quickly consider which one will enable you to achieve the best mark. All of this should be done purposefully but promptly as time is of the essence.

Exam questions use a specific vocabulary. The command words are important, because they make clear how the essay is to be approached, and you should understand what each requires of you.

Activity 2

Match the command words to their definitions in the table below.

Command word/phrase	Definition
Discuss…	Investigate a topic closely.
Evaluate…	Consider the merits of an argument or idea and whether you agree or disagree with them.
Explore…	Identify and give an account of the similarities and differences of two things.
Examine…	Investigate all the issues relating to a topic, reaching a conclusion.
How does…	Make a judgement, weighing up the strengths and weaknesses.
To what extent do you…	Write about the topic in detail, providing a considered and balanced review of the related arguments.
Compare and contrast…	Organise information into component parts and then investigate each in great detail.
Analyse…	Demonstrate the way in which the writer employs their craft.

Understanding the demands of the question

Look below at how two students have carefully considered what their questions demand.

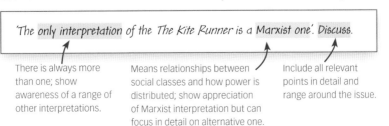

'The only interpretation of the The Kite Runner is a Marxist one'. Discuss.

There is always more than one; show awareness of a range of other interpretations.

Means relationships between social classes and how power is distributed; show appreciation of Marxist interpretation but can focus in detail on alternative one.

Include all relevant points in detail and range around the issue.

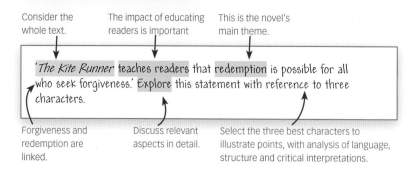

Consider the whole text.

The impact of educating readers is important

This is the novel's main theme.

'*The Kite Runner* teaches readers that redemption is possible for all who seek forgiveness.' Explore this statement with reference to three characters.

Forgiveness and redemption are linked.

Discuss relevant aspects in detail.

Select the three best characters to illustrate points, with analysis of language, structure and critical interpretations.

Activity 3

Annotate the question below to show your understanding of what is being asked.

Evaluate the extent to which you believe *The Kite Runner* is just as much about America as it is about Afghanistan.

Planning a response

Having decided which question will help you achieve the best marks, it is now important that you plan your response in some detail. You must resist the urge to start writing straightaway. The best responses are planned and this can take a variety of forms depending on the nature of the question and your preferred learning style. Options include using bullet points, a spider diagram, a concept map, a grid, or annotating an extract.

The first stage in the planning process is to note down your ideas as they come and in no particular order. Then you should number them in the order you think best to give your response an appropriate structure and illustrate your argument.

Look carefully at how the student opposite has planned their initial ideas for responding to the question below.

'How does Hosseini present the theme of friendship in *The Kite Runner*?'

The student has used a spider diagram, which is quite appropriate for the type of question that asks you to focus on one particular theme (or character) and explore its presentation. A bullet point list would also work.

Intro – a key theme; the novel is negative about friendships; all friendships are compromised; ultimately Amir saves a blood relative not a friend.

Motifs are important – pomegranate tree, Shahnamah, kites; positive at first – boys are a formidable and successful team when kite fighting; Amir carves names in the tree as a sign of their friendship; they love reading the Shahnamah together; these later assume negative associations after the betrayal – Amir pelts Hassan with fruit, 'smeared in red like he'd been shot by a firing squad'; Amir is more concerned about the blue kite than Hassan who has been raped; Amir buries the copy of the Shahnamah, his birthday present from Ali and Hassan, so it is out of sight.

Rahim Khan and Baba – their friendship is compromised because they are business partners so there is a financial aspect to their friendship.

Marxist critics – oppose the master/servant relationship, which makes real friendships impossible; Hazara/Sh'ia = disempowered/marginalised as religious, uneducated and poor; Pashtun/Sunni = powerful/dominant as wealthy, non-religious and educated, 'I was a Pashtun and he was a Hazara, I was Sunni and he was Shi'a, and nothing was ever going to change that'.

Assef – makes explicit that society prevents Amir and Hassan from being friends; most evil character speaks truth, "Because to him, you're nothing but an ugly pet"; Amir acknowledges this in his relationship with Hassan; also true of Baba and Ali; friendships in Afghanistan are impossible as always compromised by something negative.

How does Hosseini present the theme of friendship in *The Kite Runner*?

Farid and Amir – not true friends either because Farid is hired and paid for what he does.

Dream during rape – Amir's id and subconscious mind takes over (psychoanalytical interpretation); Hassan as saviour in the dream heightens tension.

Amir and Hassan – complex relationship as children; they act like friends; Amir consoles Hassan when upset by soldier, "He took you for someone else"; Amir says he loves Hassan; Hassan encourages Amir as a writer, "you will be a great writer" and defends him in the street.

Amir's betrayal of Hassan is not the action of a friend – the incident tortures him into adulthood until he brings Sohrab to USA; narrative fractures with two memories and a dream interrupting the chronology of events; reflects Amir's mental turmoil (postmodern literary technique); use of present tense further disorientates readers, like Amir; language analysis here of lamb/religious sacrifice, which adds greater pathos, 'It was the look of the lamb'.

Conclusion – no friendships in America; Taheris/Baba become real friends only after the engagement; Amir saving Sohrab is not due to friendship but because he is a blood relation, "Blood is a powerful thing".

Activity 4

a) Use a table like the one below to evaluate how successful you think the spider diagram is for planning a response to the question.

Focus	Yes	Partly	No
The response will be focused on the question.			
The introduction will provide clear direction for rest of essay.			
It follows a logical structure.			
It ranges across the novel for points to discuss.			
It makes reference to contextual issues.			
It refers to different interpretations.			
It refers to the writer's use of language.			
It refers to authorial techniques such as narrative style and symbolism.			
It uses secondary characters to illustrate its points too.			
It includes short quotations as evidence.			
It has an effective conclusion.			

b) Is there anything you think should be added to the plan on page 107?

Tips for assessment

Better responses will include an introduction and a conclusion. These work well when they are short and to the point. The best introductions will answer the question and also set up the argument to be developed in the essay. A good conclusion will sum up the main points of the essay in a forceful and memorable way. Use of a quotation from the text, the writer, a critic or even a related quotation from another text can help here. Your conclusion should have impact as it is the last thing the examiner will read.

Look carefully at the exam-style question below.

> 'The real hero of *The Kite Runner* is Hassan, not Amir.' To what extent do you agree with this statement?

A student has planned a possible response using a grid divided into separate sections. Given the nature of the question, which is asking them to argue their point of view, this seems quite appropriate because it allows the student to demonstrate their understanding of why some might believe the statement but to then go on to challenge it. The grid also shows how many paragraphs there will be.

<u>Intro</u>

- Quote Hosseini (and refer to in conclusion): '[Amir] is a better protagonist for the novel... than Hassan, who is so firmly rooted in goodness and integrity. There was a lot more room for character development with Amir than Hassan.'
- Amir is ultimately the hero due to his greater journey; Bildungsroman genre; Hassan is heroic but ultimately too good/saintly (examples of his loyalty)

<u>Arguments for the statement: Hassan is the hero</u>

1) Hassan bears disadvantage without complaint; incredible loyalty; motif of phrase *'For you, a thousand times over'*.

2) His ability to forgive despite having name smeared; 'you will find an old faithful friend waiting for you'; the novel is named after him

<u>Arguments against the statement: Amir is the hero</u>

3) First-person narrative. Amir also suffers despite his privileges: loss of his mother is made worse by his father's rejection, which he overhears, 'I hadn't turned out like him. Not at all'; Oedipus complex and psychoanalytic interpretation; stunted emotionally by events

4) Hassan's rape is traumatic for Amir too: fractured narrative/gripped by fear/ruled by the id/lamb symbol and sacrifice language; Judas reference; 'I felt paralysed' and 'I was still biting down on my fist'; he is burdened by the guilt throughout life

5) Amir displays bravery to go back to Kabul; instinct tells him not to; super ego now in play; maturing/suffers the beating, 'The knuckles shattering my jaw. Choking on my own teeth'; present tense and grammatically incorrect sentences reflecting horror of situation and sense of immediate chaos

6) Amir seeks forgiveness/assumes role of father/is redeemed; his emotional, psychological and physical journey is greater

<u>Conclusion</u>

- Amir is now a kite runner too/also a father/matured. Amir is Afghanistan and why – ethnic tensions/suffers trauma/points the way forward. Refer back to opening quotation for impact – Hosseini wants Amir to be the hero

Activity 5

Using the plan above, write the response.

Tips for assessment

Having taken the time to complete your plan, it is important that you follow it. This does not mean that you cannot adjust it as you progress. As you write, you will get other ideas that are relevant and these can be included too. Similarly, as you work through your plan, you may realise that one or two of the points are not as relevant as you first thought, so leave these out.

Writing a response

Selecting and using supporting quotations

It is vital that you use carefully selected quotations to support your ideas. These act as evidence and make clear to the examiner how you are thinking. With the exception of your introduction and possibly your conclusion, there should not be a single paragraph in your response without a number of quotations included in it. How you incorporate these is also important. Literary critics skilfully weave their supporting quotations into their writing and you should do the same.

Selecting the right supporting quotations should also be a springboard for further analysis of character, theme and, more importantly, language. An examiner will be very interested in your appreciation of how words and phrases deliberately chosen by the writer impact on readers.

Your exam may be open or closed book. Either way it is advisable that you learn some key quotations for use in your response. This will save time. Some quotations are short and very easy to remember, including, for example:

- *'For you, a thousand times over'* (Chapter 1)
- 'my past of unatoned sins' (Chapter 1)
- 'Your father, like you, was a tortured soul' (Chapter 23)
- 'I am wrestling the bear' (Chapter 23).

The quotations above are also flexible, so they can be included in response to a range of questions, testing everything from understanding of character to theme and critical interpretations.

Activity 6

Make a list of short quotations that are easy to memorise for use in your responses.

Quality of written expression

The examiner will expect you to communicate in a clear and sophisticated way. Think of your essay as a piece of literary criticism that another student might read in order to better understand the novel. In this context, you are the critic and should use a suitably formal and literary style of writing that clearly expresses complex ideas, using the correct terminology. Reading a wide range of related criticism and revising and redrafting your work regularly are two ways in which you can develop the type of style that will help you secure the higher grades.

Look closely at how the student below has revised and improved the quality of their written expression in a short passage from an essay responding to the question below.

> *'The Kite Runner* teaches readers that redemption is possible for all who seek forgiveness.' Explore this statement with reference to three characters.

educates

imploring

self-healing

juxtaposes

extremism

It is Rahim Khan who ~~tells~~ Amir about the importance of forgiveness, ~~asking~~ him to forgive himself above all else, so that the process of ~~getting better~~ can begin. His attitude ~~contrasts~~ that of the ~~strictness~~ of the Taliban, who cannot even forgive a teenager for wearing his jeans slung low enough for his underwear to show.

Spelling, punctuation and grammar

Exam responses, even though they are written under the pressure of time, obviously require legible handwriting and accurate spelling, punctuation and grammar. *The Kite Runner* presents specific challenges, given its emphasis on Afghan culture and the use of words from multiple languages. Foreign words must be spelt correctly too.

Activity 7

Look at the last piece of extended writing you did about *The Kite Runner*. Read it and correct any mistakes in spelling, grammar and punctuation, while also improving the quality of expression.

Sample questions

1 'The Kite Runner* illustrates the danger in keeping secrets.' To what extent do you agree with this statement?

2 Discuss how Hosseini presents the theme of brotherhood in *The Kite Runner*.

3 Explore the significance of setting and the way it is presented in *The Kite Runner*.

4 'The Kite Runner* is best interpreted as a coming-of-age text rather than a political one.' To what extent do you agree with this view? Remember to refer in detail to Hosseini's authorial methods.

5 Evaluate the extent to which you believe *The Kite Runner* is a misogynist text.

6 Examine how religion is presented in the novel as a positive or negative force.

Sample answers

Sample answer 1

The extract below is the start of an answer to the following exam-style question.

> 'The real hero of *The Kite Runner* is Hassan, not Amir.' To what extent do you agree with this statement?

When we consider that Hosseini himself has said – '[Amir] is a better protagonist for the novel… than Hassan, who is so firmly rooted in goodness and integrity. There was a lot more room for character development with Amir than Hassan' – it is difficult to agree that Hassan is the real hero in *The Kite Runner*.

Shows research; quotation powerfully supports the argument.

There is no doubt that Hassan is a heroic figure. He is the embodiment of loyalty, sacrificing himself for Amir despite the consequences and in ways only a saint would. How he stoically bears his disadvantage, is able to forgive and embraces fatherhood so completely are all further indications of a man who is an example to all. As the kite runner in the story, the novel is also named after him. However, characters are deliberate creations and, as the quotation above makes clear, Hassan, if anything, is too good, too saintly. It was clearly Hosseini's intention that Amir be the hero, given his flaws and the difficulty of his journey to redemption.

Shows clear understanding of why some might believe Hassan is heroic.

Written in strong, confident style.

Understands characters are constructs that serve the writer's purpose.

Links back to the opening quotation.

Understands the writer's intention.

Amir, despite his considerable privilege, endures a challenging childhood. His mother is dead and deeply missed, a fact made worse by the mistaken belief that he is culpable for her death. His father is distant, aloof and ashamed of his son, something which Amir is fully aware of: 'I hadn't turned out like him. Not at all.' This generates sympathy for the boy, which the first-person narrative approach is designed to foster. Amir's emotional development is at risk here if a psychological reading of the text is applied. Unable to truly experience and process the Oedipal stage of his development, as his mother was not physically present in his life, Amir is emotionally stunted as a result of growing up without a mother.

Uses sophisticated vocabulary.

A short, pertinent quotation used to good effect.

Fully appreciates the type of narrator employed.

Understands the psychoanalytic interpretation.

This relates to his abandonment of Hassan later in the alley. A more sympathetic approach to Amir's character might argue that his refusal to help Hassan is stimulated by fear, which is understandable given the level of violence he has witnessed Assef dish out to others previously.

However, as Amir himself admits, it also stems from a desire to ingratiate himself with a father who has publically expressed his shame in him through word and deed: 'Baba's valiant efforts to conceal the disgusted look on his face […] "There is something missing in that boy."' Hassan suffers a terrible and sickening injustice at the hands of Assef, but Amir suffers too. Of course, this is not to the same extent as Hassan, but the postmodern techniques employed,

Fully understands post-modernist techniques and their impact.

Appreciates the writer is manipulating language and its impact.

Psychoanalytic interpretation is reflected again; shows good understanding of text and the writer's intentions.

Comments on the language.

Acknowledges social context of the novel.

Uses an apt biblical reference.

such as the insertion of two memories and a dream, which disrupt and fragment the chronology, are designed to represent a child's mind in turmoil. The fact that two of these are expressed using the present tense add further to Amir's and readers' feelings of disorientation.

Amir's actions here are dominated by his id as his instinct is in overdrive and tells him to protect himself above all else. However, his closed eyes, tears and the blood drawn by biting down on his hand reflect the emotional and physical pain being endured by Hassan simultaneously, uniting the two boys despite their different circumstances. Amir recalls the Eid-Al-Adha lamb sacrifice and identifies Hassan's face with that of 'the lamb'. This is an important religious image of youth and innocence. Lambs are defenceless and easy prey for more sinister forces. Amir is subconsciously acknowledging how ethnic and religious divisions within Afghan society render Hassan powerless, not only against the three Pashtun boys restraining him but also against Amir's self-interest and all its consequences. More importantly, Amir is framing his betrayal of Hassan as a sacrifice to echo another great betrayal – that of Jesus by Judas. This is revisited later, when Amir describes the rain on the windows as Baba drives Ali and Hassan to the bus station as 'melting silver', which recalls the 30 pieces of silver paid to Judas. Such imagery and associations imbue a terrible situation with even greater potency, dramatic tension and pathos.

This strong response shows an in-depth understanding of the novel and the demands of the question. The student writes in a very confident style, expressing themselves with sophisticated language and using the tone of a literary critic. There is appropriate reference to the authorial techniques involved, with clear appreciation of how structural devices and language are used to develop meaning. Understanding of a psychoanalytic interpretation underpins the analysis. References to contextual issues and the Bible are apt and well integrated. Use of the quotation by Hosseini backs up the student's argument. To achieve a higher-band response, it is important that this student now addresses the rest of the plan on page 109 in order to further demonstrate why Amir is the novel's real hero.

Activity 8

Use the rest of the plan to complete the response.

Sample answer 2

The extract below is the start of an answer to the following exam-style question.

> 'In *The Kite Runner*, Hosseini makes it clear that where social inequality exists, only conflict follows.' To what extent do you agree with this view? Remember to include in your answer relevant detailed exploration of Hosseini's authorial methods.

Hosseini's novel is a celebration of Afghanistan, its people and its culture, but it is also a condemnation of the inequality, sectarianism and violence inherent in that country. It furthermore establishes that this will continue if the individual silently accepts it.

Clear overview reveals student's opinion.

The relationships between Amir and Baba and Ali and Hassan best illustrate the social inequality that lies at the heart of the contemporary Afghan society, an equality that is exacerbated by ethnic and religious differences. Baba and Amir are members of the ruling Pashtun group and are Sunni Muslims, while Ali and Hassan are Hazaras and Shi'a. The former are wealthy, privileged and live a Western lifestyle during the reign of Zahir Khan, while the latter are disempowered, humble, poor servants. Within a Marxist context, Baba represents the bourgeoisie and his capitalist ventures make him 'one of the richest merchants in Kabul'. This allows conspicuous consumption such as the 'marble floors [...] intricate mosaic tiles [and] gold stitched tapestries' found in his home, which is situated in 'a new and affluent neighbourhood'.

Sophisticated vocabulary and expression.

Understands context.

Further contextual comment.

Links question to Marxist interpretation.

Well-selected quotations woven into analysis.

In contrast, Ali and Hassan live in third world conditions, 'a mud shack' with only the essentials. Before the Saur Revolution of 1978, Baba throws lavish parties, drinks alcohol and smokes. He can take a month off work to fly to Tehran and watch the World Cup and has the money to fund and build an orphanage. Baba can openly lambast religious leaders as 'bearded idiots' and his sphere of influence is such that Amir is exempt from the corporal punishment meted out at school. On the other hand, Ali and Hassan are poor, deeply religious and illiterate. This enables the bourgeoisie to maintain power over them. Religious devotion makes Ali and Hassan too accepting of their situation and too forgiving of the wrongs inflicted on them. Their lack of education makes them too blind to the exploitative system they live in and unable to articulate their grievances. Their quiet acceptance of their situation echoes the caste system found in Afghanistan so embedded in their psyche is their sense of servitude.

Understands context.

Very good knowledge of the text here.

Clearly understands the social inequality present in the novel.

The resulting conflict is multi-layered: figures of authority casually denigrate the Hazaras, such as Amir's teacher who '…wrinkled his nose when he said the word Shi'a like it was like some form of disease'; Baba brings disruption to Ali's marriage, satisfying his own lust; Amir himself, through his first-person, retrospective, limited narration reveals a different

Appreciates choice of narrative voice.

Punctuation used skilfully here to explain how conflict emerges in different ways.

type of conflict, an inner one that he feels in regards to Hassan, torn as he is between his feelings of friendship on the one hand and innate superiority on the other: 'I was a Pashtun and he was a Hazara... and nothing was ever going to change that.'

Awareness of critical interpretations.

However, the most odious conflict arising from this inequality is the violence inflicted on the minority Hazara by the majority Pashtun. This is the natural outworking of the sectarianism which permeates society and is evident in the rape of Hassan by Assef. Hosseini makes the setting for this horrific attack an alleyway, suggesting the baseness of the perpetrator and the act. Some critics interpret this event in allegorical terms with Hassan representing Afghanistan, Assef the USSR and Amir the passive international community. The sexual violence implied in the phallic symbolism, 'part the curtain... embedded in deep twin craters...

Appreciates language.

deflated cheeks' is permissible according to Assef because, 'It's just a Hazara.' He sees Hassan as less than human because society has nurtured

Contextual references.

in him the belief that the Hazaras 'pollute' Afghanistan. Amir justifies his failure to intervene with, 'He was just a Hazara' – an echo of Assef's words, aligning both in their prejudice. Such violence escalates with the onset of civil war and the subsequent rise of Islamic extremism. Assef's sociopathic tendencies find a home in the Taliban and the persecution of the Hazara becomes mass murder at Mazar-i-Sharif. Assef's delight in the memory makes clear the depths of his delusion and derangement: '...let the bullets

Links neatly back to the question and introduction.

fly, free of guilt and remorse, knowing you are virtuous, good, and decent.' On this occasion, however, the adult Amir does not remain silent and challenges Assef, 'They call it ethnic cleansing', which is indicative of the bravery required to create a fairer and more just Afghanistan.

This response reveals an excellent understanding of the novel and is analytical in nature. It establishes the nature of the inequality and its consequences. Written in a critical style, it uses a sophisticated vocabulary and expression. There is a very good appreciation of different interpretations, context and language use. Ideas are supported by carefully-selected supporting quotations. This response would be placed in the highest band.

Sample answer 3

The extract below is the start of an answer to the following exam-style question.

> Analyse the ways relationships between fathers and sons are presented in
> *The Kite Runner*.

Amir has a difficult relationship with his father. His dad is a very popular and successful businessman. He is well liked in his local community. Baba is also a very strong man. He likes sports such as soccer and buzkashi, which is very dangerous. He is everything an Afghan male is supposed to be, even putting himself in danger by standing up to the Russian soldier who is about to rape a woman. Amir is very different though. He is not physically strong. Hassan has to stick up for him, when other kids in the street pick on him, like when he prevented Assef from attacking Amir with his slingshot. I feel sad for Amir, who has lost his mum and feels distant from his father. He tries his best to play soccer but is useless at it. When he goes to the buzkashi, it makes him cry because it is so violent and one of the riders dies. Amir is more interested in reading and writing, which also annoys his dad, who feels that these things have little value. Amir hears his father tell Rahim Khan, "If I hadn't seen the doctor pull him out of my wife with my own eyes, I'd never believe he's my son." This is a terrible thing for a child to hear his father say and creates sympathy for Amir.

Ali has a much more loving relationship with his son Hassan, even though he is not his biological father. They are very happy with their life as servants and also very religious. After the rape, Ali asks Amir if anything happened to Hassan, which shows he is worried about him. Ali also stands up to Baba and tells him they are leaving when Baba orders him to stay. This shows that he wants to protect Hassan as much as he can and be the best father he can be. I like Ali and think he did a good job rearing Hassan. He could not give him very much like Baba does Amir, but he gives him all the love that he has and he has taught him to be a good person.

Hassan is also a good father to Sohrab. Again, although they are very poor, there is a real love between them. Hassan and Sohrab do the very same things that Hassan and Amir did as children. They go to the cinema, visit the pomegranate tree, read the *shahnamah* and fly kites together. I think it is very interesting that Hassan teaches Sohrab to use a slingshot

Annotations:

An overview of the student's intentions for the essay might be beneficial here.

Shows knowledge of the text and some contextual awareness, but uses no supporting quotations.

Recognises the contrast.

Shows good knowledge of text but uses no supporting quotations; fails to include discussion of the lack of strong female influence during Amir's childhood.

Accurately uses a relevant supporting quotation.

Shows awareness of the impact on readers.

Makes relevant points but in a rather basic way, lacking sophisticated expression.

Comparison between Baba's wealth and Ali's love here is a better, more analytical point.

Omits the capital 'S' and misses the opportunity to discuss the symbolic importance of the book.

Misses opportunity to discuss the symbolic importance of the tree.

Misses opportunity to develop this and discuss ethnic tensions and Marxist criticism.

Quotation is too long and only reiterates earlier paraphrasing; misses opportunity to discuss use of parallels in the narrative and also use of symbolism.

because he knows that his son will need it to protect himself in life, and he also teaches Sohrab to read and write, which Hassan could not do as a child. It says, 'Hassan taught him how to shoot the slingshot, and, later, by the time he was eight, Sohrab had become deadly with that thing: He could stand on the terrace and hit a pinecone propped on a pail halfway across the yard. Hassan taught him to read and write—his son was not going to grow up illiterate like he had'. It is with slingshots that both Hassan and Sohrab save Amir from Assef.

This student demonstrates a good knowledge of the text. Spelling and punctuation are generally accurate. The paragraphs do not illustrate and support a clear line of argument. Several of the more obvious father/ son relationships are identified for discussion. However, beyond that no awareness is demonstrated of how this theme is developed through use of language and symbol, for example through further analysis of what reading and storytelling represents and Baba's disinterest in it during their time in Kabul. The changing nature of the relationship between Amir and Baba in America could also have been explored. There is a lack of carefully selected, short supporting quotations, which could have facilitated language analysis. This response would be placed in the lower mark bands.

Activity 9

Rewrite and improve the response using the annotations and summary comment to help you.

Glossary

allegory a story, poem or painting in which the characters and events are symbols of something else, often political, religious or moral

allusion a brief reference, which might be social, cultural, literary, political or historical

anthropomorphised when non-human creatures are given human attributes

autobiographical about the writer's own life and experiences

catharsis the act of releasing intense or repressed emotions

confessional revealing private thoughts or events that have happened that might be considered shameful or a secret

direct address when a writer talks directly to readers through the use of words like 'you' and 'your'

epic poetry long narrative poems set in the past and involving heroic characters and supernatural forces or gods

epistolary written in letters

first-person narration the voice of a narrator who tells the story from their own point of view

gerund the form of the verb ending in -*ing*

high culture referring to art forms, such as classical music, enjoyed by highly educated people

idiolect the unique speech habits and patterns of an individual

literary realism a movement in literature and art to present familiar things as they really are

low culture referring to popular art forms, such as pop music, enjoyed by ordinary people

lyricism the use of heightened, poetic language to express deep emotions

metafiction a piece of fiction consciously telling a story and deliberately reminding readers of this

metaphor a direct comparison in which one thing is said to be another

misogynistic prejudiced against women

modernism a movement away from traditional forms or ideas, reconsidering what is meant by realism and influenced by psychological ideas

mythology the study of ancient tales and stories relating to a specific religion or culture

non-linear narrative a story that is not told chronologically and includes flashbacks and/or flash-forwards

omniscient all-knowing

pathetic fallacy a type of personification in which nature is given human characteristics to reflect the action and generate atmosphere

phallic symbolism the use of objects to symbolise the male sexual organs

postmodernism a concept in art and literature that developed against modernism, distrusting theories and systems of ideas

psychoanalytic analysis relating to the study of how personality is organised and developed

redemption the action of saving, or being saved from, sin, error or evil

redemption arc the journey of a character from bad to good

Romanticism a movement in literature and art that celebrated imagination, emotion and the natural world

rule of three a three-part structure designed to emphasise a point

sectarianism discrimination from religious intolerance

stream of consciousness a narrative approach where the inner thoughts of an individual are communicated in a continuous flow

subplot the secondary events or storylines that run parallel to the main plots, reflecting, underpinning and developing them

symbolic something that represents something else, e.g. red roses are symbolic of love

symbolic importance significant because of what things represent

Great Clarendon Street, Oxford, OX2 6DP, United Kingdom

Oxford University Press is a department of the University of Oxford. It
furthers the University's objective of excellence in research, scholarship,
and education by publishing worldwide. Oxford is a registered trade mark
of Oxford University Press in the UK and in certain other countries

British Library Cataloguing in Publication Data

Data available

ISBN 978-019843748-2

Kindle edition ISBN 978-019843751-2

10 9 8 7 6 5 4 3 2 1

Printed in Hong Kong by Sheck Wah Tong Printing Press Ltd.

Acknowledgements

We are grateful for the permission to reprint the following copyright
texts:

Excerpts from Khaled Hosseini: *The Kite Runner*, (Bloomsbury, 2011).
© Khaled Hosseini, 2011, *The Kite Runner*, Bloomsbury Publishing Plc.
Reproduced with permission from Bloomsbury Publishing Plc.

E. Milvy: *The Kite Runner Controversy*, Salon, 9 December
(Salon Magazine, 2007).

We have tried to trace and contact all copyright holders before
publication. If notified, the publishers will be pleased to rectify any errors
or omissions at the earliest opportunity.

The publisher and authors would like to thank the following for
permission to use photographs and other copyright material:

Cover: Barcroft Media; **p7:** TCD/Prod.DB/Alamy Stock Photo; **p16:**
Nicholas Burningham/Alamy Stock Photo; **p24:** Michael Tran/Getty
Images; **p26:** Scott Peterson /Getty Images; **p27:** Insights/Getty Images;
p32: US Army Photo/Alamy Stock Photo; **p33:** Paula Bronstein/Getty
Images; **p37:** Moviestore collection Ltd/Alamy Stock Photo; **p41:**
Entertainment Pictures/Alamy Stock Photo; **p48:** TCD/Prod.DB/Alamy
Stock Photo; **p52:** TCD/Prod.DB/Alamy Stock Photo; **p56:** Entertainment
Pictures/Alamy Stock Photo; **p59:** Entertainment Pictures/Alamy Stock
Photo; **p66:** Xinhua/Alamy Stock Photo; **p73:** Entertainment Pictures/
Alamy Stock Photo; **p76:** Sajjad Nayan/Alamy Stock Photo; **p83:** AFP/Getty
Images; **p84:** Roger Lemoyne/Getty Images; **p92:** TCD/Prod.DB/Alamy
Stock Photo; **p99:** Paula Bronstein/Getty Images.

Artwork by Lovell Johns (p25).

Every effort has been made to contact copyright holders of material
reproduced in this book. Any omissions will be rectified in subsequent
printings if notice is given to the publisher.